m

ALSO BY ROSETTA LOY

The Dust Roads of Monferrato

FIRST WORDS

ROSETTA LOY

FIRST WORDS

A CHILDHOOD IN FASCIST ITALY

Translated by Gregory Conti

Metropolitan Books

HENRY HOLT AND COMPANY   NEW YORK

Metropolitan Books
Henry Holt and Company
Publishers since 1866
115 West 18th Street
New York, New York 10011

Metropolitan Books is an imprint of
Henry Holt and Company.

Published in Canada by Fitzhenry and Whiteside Ltd.,
195 Allstate Parkway, Markham, Ontario L3R 4T8

Originally published in Italy in 1997 under the title *La parola ebreo*
by Giulio Einaudi editore s.p.a., Turin. All rights reserved.

First published in the United States in 2000 by Henry Holt and Company.

Library of Congress Cataloging-in-Publication Data
Loy, Rosetta, 1931–
[Parola ebreo. English]
First words : a childhood in Fascist Italy / Rosetta Loy ; translated by Gregory
Conti.
p.   cm.
ISBN 0-8050-6258-0
1. Jews—Persecutions—Italy. 2. Holocaust, Jewish (1939–1945)—Italy—
Personal narratives. 3. World War, 1939–1945—Catholic Church. 4. Italy—
Ethnic relations. 5. Loy, Rosetta, 1931– —Childhood and youth. I. Title.

DS135.I8 L6913 2000
940.53'18'0945—dc21   00-021877

First American Edition 2000

Designed by Kate Nichols

Printed in the United States of America
1   3   5   7   9   10   8   6   4   2

FIRST WORDS

1 9 3 6

IF I GO BACK IN TIME and think of when I first heard the word *Jew*, I see myself sitting on a little blue chair in the nursery, a room with flowery peach-colored wallpaper showing the marks of children's scribbles. It is late spring and the high window facing the stone terrace is wide open. I can look into the apartment on the other side of the street and see the curtains there swinging in the breeze. Inside there's a party going on; I can watch the people coming and going. Just a few days ago, the family had a new baby and the party is for him. I turn to the woman sitting beside me, also on a small chair, her body wrapped up like a ball.

"Is it a baptism?" I ask her.

"Certainly not," she says. She is Annemarie, my German nanny, my *fräulein*. "They are Jews," she adds, gesturing toward the window with her chin. "They don't baptize their babies, they circumcise them," she explains, using the German, *beschneiden,* with a grimace of disgust. I haven't learned the word, but I know part of it, *schneiden,* to cut.

"What?" I say, not believing her.

"Yes, they cut off a piece of the flesh," she tells me matter of factly.

"With scissors?" I picture the blood, a sea of red washing over the bassinet. Annemarie's explanation is vague but chilling. She indicates some part of the body as she peers out the window with a severe look on her face, but I don't understand her gesture. "Yes," she says, "really, with scissors."

Inside the apartment across the street I can see little girls with bows in their hair just like mine, and ladies wearing pearl necklaces, draped in soft knit dresses like the ones my mother wears.

"They are Jews," Annemarie says again, and her beautiful sky-blue eyes turn harsh as her gaze rests on a maid walking through the room with a tray in her hands. Perhaps there among the teacups is the piece that was cut off the new baby, a lump of skin or even a whole finger.

Our neighbor, Signora Della Seta, is also Jewish. She lives next door and is old, or at least she seems old to me. One day when I'm sick she comes to visit. I have a fever and am lying in my mother's room in the huge double bed, where my body is all but swallowed up. Signora Della Seta's gray hair is rolled up in a net. She has a present for me, a little basket lined with blue satin; inside is a baby doll held in place by elastic strips sewn into the satin. Another strip holds a tiny baby's bottle with a red tip. I think it's a beautiful present; there's also a doll-sized pair of underpants and a sweater. I love Signora Della Seta, even though she's Jewish.

Our upstairs neighbors are the Levis. They are noisy. Sometimes I can hear them playing the piano. Their mother has very dark bright eyes. The Levis are not kind like Signora Della Seta and we see them only on the stairs or in the elevator. They don't bring me presents. Annemarie says they are Jewish as well. Every so often Giorgio Levi rings our doorbell and asks my brother to play soccer with him in the Villa Borghese. Giorgio is a year older than my brother. He has dark wavy hair and the cheerful face of a boy who lives to race down the stairs to play outside with his friends. After the game, my brother comes back and washes his feet in the bidet. He complains that Giorgio is bossy and if he doesn't pass him the ball fast enough, Giorgio elbows him in the side.

At kindergarten, Mother Gregoria shows us the color illustrations in the Bible. She has round red cheeks. She's small and she, too, sits in a little chair, the folds of her long white wool dress spread out on the floor. Embroidered over her breast is a pierced red heart worn in memory of the Passion of Christ. In her chubby little hands she holds up a picture of Abraham raising his sword over Isaac, his son. Luckily an angel comes in time to stop him from killing Isaac. Abraham and Isaac are Jews also; they chose to die in the flames rather than deny God. In those days God had no heart, then luckily Christ came down to earth. Unlike God, Christ is beautiful and good. He has long chestnut hair and blue eyes. Every morning when I go to kindergarten he is there waiting for me. His pink plaster hand points to the heart exposed on his chest, which has little drops of blood dripping from it. The heart is where love is. Christ loves us.

We are Christians—I was baptized in Saint Peter's and my godmother is Signora Basile. She's old like Signora Della Seta but she's a lot skinnier; her long neck and small head make her look like an ostrich. One time when she came to visit, my brother opened the door to the living room, where she was sitting, and said, "Signora Basile has a mustache," then ran away. It's true—the bristly gray hairs above her lip scratch my cheek when she leans down to kiss me. But she has very gentle round eyes, and she didn't even get angry when my brother was rude to her. He was trying to be tough. For my baptism she gave me a gold chain with the Madonna of Pompeii on a medallion that I suck on when I'm in bed in the dark. Every year at Christmas Signora Basile organizes a charity raffle for the poor people of the parish. Pilate was Roman and the Pharisees and the scribes were Jews. Herod was a Jew and so was Cain. And Barabbas. They were all Jews, except the centurions.

ON THE DAYS when I don't go to kindergarten, Annemarie takes me to the Villa Giulia to a little park tucked away beside the National Gallery of Modern Art. I'm always wrapped up in a hat and scarf because I'm not as strong as my sister Teresa. There's hardly ever anyone else in the park, but then I'm not supposed to play with other children in case I catch something from them. Sometimes there's another little girl on her own, crouched near the benches, stirring the gravel around with a colored shovel. I can see her underpants, the large white kind we call *petit bateau,* just like the ones Annemarie slips on me every morning. I squat on the gravel as well and look at her. She is blond and her wavy hair falls down around her very fair skin. I'd like to have her shovel. Around her neck she wears a gold star. Annemarie calls to me. She's talking to the other girl's nanny. They say that the girl is very rich. Maybe I can play with her. I turn back to look at her as she stirs the gravel and am fascinated by her star as it dangles in the sun, reflecting sparks of light. I ask her whether I can touch it. "No, you can't," she says. She doesn't want me to come too close. As we walk home, I ask Annemarie about the star. "It's the Star of David," she tells me. Mother Gregoria has shown us a picture of David slinging stones at Goliath. Annemarie explains that the girl wears a six-pointed star instead of a Blessed Mother medallion or one of baby Jesus. I don't know how, but I understand that the girl is Jewish without Annemarie's telling me. "Did they cut her, too?" I say. "What do you mean? Cut what?" Annemarie is speaking German. I have to speak German as well, otherwise she won't answer me. Now the star seems full of mystery. I'm jealous of the girl who can wear that instead of my plain old medallion.

I have a book about the adventures of a little Catholic boy kidnapped by unbelievers who want him to renounce Jesus. In the book there are some Freemasons who are very wicked. The boy is taken to a ship where there is a Jew, and he's very wicked, too. They all want to take away the boy's faith but he prays to the Blessed Mother and resists. At a certain point he is almost blinded. I don't like that book, it's cruel and stupid. I like the book about the sandman who sprinkles silver dust on the eyelids of sleeping children and carries them off to the Land of Dreams. I also like the book where you see the Befana at night, struggling to make her way through the snow and sliding down the chimney into the houses. I believe in the Befana, even though it never snows in Rome and we don't have a chimney.

THAT'S ME in the winter of 1936. But before I go back to the little girl on the blue chair looking intently out the window, I want for a moment to step back even further, to 1931, the year IX of the Fascist era, when that little girl is born in our house at 21 via Flaminia in the red room, named for its wine-colored carpet. A few days after her birth, as raindrops slither down the windows of the family car, the girl is taken to the Saint Peter's Basilica to be baptized. She is accompanied by her brother and two sisters, along with their nannies and governess (the brother is four, the youngest sister just fifteen months). At the baptismal font she is given the name Pia, together with several other names, in honor of Pius XI, the reigning pope.

In November of that year, the Ministry of Public Affairs issues a circular requiring university professors to swear an oath of loyalty to Fascism. Of 1,200 professors, 1,188 agree to take the oath and pledge to teach according to the principles of Fascist doctrine; only 12 professors prefer to give up their positions.

Also in that year, Giovanni Papini, a well-known and respected writer, publishes a new novel. Papini is a

Florentine, a talented man of letters with a powerful intellect; in the early years of the century he was denounced as a heretic. Following his public conversion to Catholicism in 1921, he wrote *Storia di Cristo,* a fictionalized biography based on the legend of the Wandering Jew, who is embodied in Buttadeo, an immortal man condemned to wander the world for all eternity. To Papini, Buttadeo represents the fate of the Jews, who will forever bear the stain of Christ's blood. Despite the punishment of their exile and their isolation from mankind, the people who killed the son of God obstinately refuse to convert. Papini claims that the eternal wanderer has in fact found a refuge, a homeland "in gold." Other members of the tribe, those from "the ghettos of Slavia," are described as "filthy and oily." It is they who represent the original Buttadeo. *Storia di Cristo* provoked a great controversy when published, but it nonetheless sold seventy thousand copies in its first year and was translated into French, English, German, Polish, Spanish, Romanian, Dutch, and Finnish.

Papini's new novel, *Gog,* is a series of fictional interviews conducted by a wealthy and eccentric American businessman—the eponymous Gog—who wants to discover the hidden diseases infecting contemporary society. Gog interviews Mahatma Gandhi, Sigmund Freud, Thomas Edison, George Bernard Shaw, and a whole series of celebrated twentieth-century figures. At some point in the book, the reader encounters Benrubi, Gog's secretary and a Jewish prototype. He is described as "a short young man with slightly curved shoulders, concave cheeks, sunken eyes, his hair showing the first signs of gray, his skin the greenish color of swamp mud . . . and with the facial expression of a dog who is afraid of being beaten but who nonetheless knows that he is necessary." Answering his employer's questions about the cowardliness of the Jews, Benrubi begins a lengthy explanation of his people's preoccupation with money:

> Unable to take up iron, the Jews protected themselves with gold. . . . Having become a capitalist in self-defense, the Jew, by way of the moral and mystical decadence of Europe, has become one of the rulers of the world, . . . dominating rich and poor alike. . . . Spat on and kicked around by his enemies, how was the Jew to exact his revenge? By degrading the Gentiles, by humiliating them, unmasking and destroying their ideals, ruining the values by which Christianity claims to live. If you look closely, over the last century, Jewish intelligence has done nothing but undermine and defile your dearest beliefs. . . . Since the moment Jews were allowed to write freely your spiritual scaffolding has been threatening to collapse.

Benrubi goes on to recite a list of personalities, such as Karl Marx, Heinrich Heine, and Cesare Lombroso, who have destroyed Christian values. He concludes:

> Born among different peoples, engaged in various fields of research, German, French, Italian, and Polish, poets and mathematicians, anthropologists and philosophers, all of [the Jews] share a common character and a common goal: to cast doubt on that which we know as truth, to debase that which is lofty, to dirty that which is pure, to question that which seems solid, to vilify that which is respected.

Twelve years later, in 1943, *Gog* will feature in Radio Vichy's propaganda and the Italian Republic of Salo will adopt the book for use in a course on anti-Semitism at the officers' training school.

Although Papini is highly regarded by my family, and *Storia di Cristo* and *Gog* have their place on the bookshelf alongside the biography of Napoleon and novels by Paul Bourget and Antonio Fogazzaro, my family is neither Fascist nor even racist. There are a few books that might suggest otherwise, such as those by the priest Ugo Mioni, which, despite their evident anti-Semitic inspiration, are read aloud to us children. But the respect given these books is certainly based on religious considerations.

My father went to a boarding school run by the Barnabite monks of Lodi; he entered at age ten and left eight years later, his only break twenty days of vacation each year spent with his family. His stories about his school years thrill us and leave us feeling vaguely anxious at the same time. He conjures up pictures of boys lined up on their dormitory beds, waiting for the servants to pull off their black boots. The servants pull so hard that the boys slide off their beds onto the floor, and it always feels like their feet are being pulled off along with their boots. He recalls washing in the mornings with a pitcher of water, a layer of ice frozen across the surface. He tells of playing cops and robbers, a game permitted only so long as the boys don't touch one another: touching is forbidden. In the game they are allowed to tap one another with a stiff rope that has been put out to freeze in the courtyard; the rope, which becomes hard as a cane, is used savagely by the bigger boys to beat their younger schoolmates. He talks of the eternal wait for his mother's monthly visit and of the cold and darkness of foggy mornings that make him feel so sad he claims to be sick and spends the day without eating, all alone in the infirmary.

He was an irreverent and undisciplined boy who played hooky from school to go swimming in the River Po. But before long he was transformed into a model student. At his graduation he received an honorable mention, a distinction that involved having his portrait in oil hung in the school gallery. Then it was on to the Polytechnic Institute in Turin, to his passion for engineering and his discovery of politics. Almost immediately, he and his best friend, Fioravanti, joined the anti-Fascist Catholic Popular Party, led by Father Luigi Sturzo. Fortunately, my father was exempt from military service on medical grounds.

He was allergic to Fascism from its inception. By 1919, when Benito Mussolini founded the National Fascist Party, he was a licensed engineer who had already made a name for himself constructing houses, bridges, and roads. He optimistically believed that Fascism would turn out to be a mere brushfire. Even after Mussolini's appointment as prime minister in 1922, even after Giacomo Matteotti, his Socialist deputy, was assassinated by Fascist thugs, my father still hoped Mussolini would soon fall. Instead, the Fascists only became stronger. To put a stop to the interminable chatter of the Fascist enthusiasts who came to his office he put up a sign in the waiting room that said, "In this office we do not talk politics." He married late; my mother is thirteen years younger than he.

Eventually, like the vast majority of Italians, he had to register as a member of the National Fascist Party in order to be able to continue working; now he wears the party symbol in his jacket lapel. However, he doesn't own a single uniform. On those rare occasions when he has to put on a black shirt for the official opening of a construction site or for a dignitary's visit to some road or bridge, we children watch in delight as he stands in front of the mirror mimicking the gestures and attitudes of the Fascists. Fioravanti, his friend from Turin Polytechnic, prefers to work abroad rather than sign up with the party.

One of my mother's best friends is married to a Jew, Baron Castelnuovo, and Signora Della Seta, our neighbor, is often in the living room taking tea, sitting in the armchair usually occupied by my godmother, Signora Basile. Mama happily shops in stores with names like Coen and Schostal, which is one of her favorites. And our pediatrician is Dr. Luzzatti, physician to the royal family and a full-blooded Jew, or *Volljude,* as Hitler would say.

For Italian Jews, the first step on the road to tragedy is in 1933 with Hitler's rise to power, when a profound shift occurs in the minds of Italy's forty million citizens. With his appointment to the chancellery, the emblems of Italian Fascism, its discipline and fervor, are conflated with the deathly racial program of the Nazi swastika, and religiously inspired anti-Semitism (which in all probability would have died down over time) is now bolstered by quasi-utopian hatred and fanaticism.

This is also the year the Catholic Church and the Third Reich agree on a concordat, which confirmed supreme papal power over the Catholic clergy in Germany and gave generous privileges to church institutions; in exchange, the Catholic Church in Germany withdrew from political and social involvement. The document is negotiated and signed by Vatican Secretary of State Cardinal Eugenio Pacelli. At its meeting on July 14, the Council of Reich Ministers discusses the concordat and, according to the minutes, Adolf Hitler, ruler of more than thirty million German Catholics, expresses his sense of relief: "This agreement, whose content does not interest me in the least, has created an area of trust that will be very useful in the developing struggle against international Jewry."

German bishops welcome the concordat, believing that it will protect them from Nazi reprisals and enable many of them to sympathize openly with the leader of the new Germany. The only bishop to disassociate himself from the agreement is Michael von Faulhaber of Munich, who speaks against the oppression of Jews from the pulpit of his cathedral, where he will be buried many years later. His Advent homilies on "Judaism, Christianity, and Germanism" are attended by a crowd of the faithful so large that loudspeakers are installed to allow him to be heard in two other churches. But Faulhaber's talks have no echo. His dissent remains an isolated protest and German officials do not feel compelled to take a position against him. (In Italy, Faulhaber's homilies are published in 1934 by Morecelliana, a Catholic publisher. They are translated by

Father Giuseppe Ricciotti, who also writes an eloquent preface protesting Germany's racial policies.)

Catholics in France are more outspoken. This is evident in the writings and speeches of the priests Jacques Maritain, Oscar de Ferenzy, and Marie-André Dieux. In April 1933 at a demonstration in support of German Jews, Dieux declares that it is necessary "to make reparation . . . for the injustices committed in the past by those who professed the same faith I do." Not to delude ourselves: such demonstrations are isolated events even in France. The majority of clerics and Church faithful are unaware; they hear nothing but the vaguely muffled sound of discrimination.

BUT TO RETURN to the little girl sitting beside her fräulein, Annemarie, in the room with the flowery peach wallpaper. Annemarie is copying illustrations from a German children's book. She's very good at drawing. Her pencil copies the outline of Nikolas, who is dunking some children in a bottle of ink for making fun of a little black boy because of the color of his skin. When the children are pulled from the giant bottle, they are black from the tops of their heads to the soles of their shoes; each child holds a doughnut that is equally black. They fall happily into line behind the black boy, whom you can no longer tell apart from the others.

Later in the afternoon, when my brother has finished his homework, my sisters and I march behind him around the edge of the hall carpet singing a popular song from 1935, when Italy invaded Abyssinia:

> *Little black face,*
> *Abyssinian dear,*
> *Keep waiting and hoping,*
> *The hour is near.*

We take turns wearing the only fez we have, made of purple cloth with a straggly tassel hanging from the crown.

Our musical repertoire is best displayed in the spring, on our annual trip to Ostia, where we breathe the sea air that is so good for our lungs. During the drive our voices find release in boisterous patriotic anthems. As we pass the beech trees on the sea road and Francesco, our driver, closes the glass partition to avoid being deafened, we move from the triumphant strains of "O sun that rises free and merry, on our hills your horses tame" to the repeated verses of "You'll never see anything greater than Rome, greater than Rome." This song always seems very sad to me because the word for "greater"— *maggiore*—also means "major," and I think that the major of Rome (who ranks below our Duce, marshal of the empire) has in some way disgraced himself and is

languishing behind bars, condemned never to see anything ever again. But the moment always arrives for a
rousing chorus:

> *Rome claims her empire,*
> *It is the hour of the eagle,*
> *Trumpet blasts salute her flight.*

From one day to the next we are forbidden to sing "Little
Black Face" and the fez is confiscated and buried among
the old toys in the trunk in the hallway. Our concierge,
Dominio, has explained to Annemarie that the song is
prohibited because its invitation to the "Abyssinian
dear" might dilute the purity of the race to which we
belong. From now on, whenever I go with our maid,
Italia, to buy bread I look apprehensively at the little
statue that stands in the bakery, a painted cast-iron figure
of a black man holding a collection box in the shape of a
house. If I slip in a coin—all it takes is ten centesimi—
the man nods his head up and down. "He's saying thank
you," the cashier tells me. To me he is now the little
black face of Abyssinia, although Italia thinks he's one of
the missionaries' Africans.

The missionaries are very important in our house. We
talk about them often and once in a while they appear in
our living room in the shape of priests with long beards
drinking coffee. They come from far away and bring

gifts of sandalwood boxes, crucifixes inlaid with mother-of-pearl, rosaries made of olive wood from Gethsemane, or tiger skins with long nails in their paws, wide-open jaws, and cold glass eyes. Before the missionaries leave they lay a hand on our heads and bless us children, and once back in Africa they send us pictures in which they are dressed in white, standing before their newly built wooden churches.

1 9 3 7

IN 1937 HITLER HAS been in power for four years. In Germany the first concentration camps have areas for political prisoners and a section for Jews, most of whom are charged with raping Aryan girls. Jews with foresight and opportunity have begun to emigrate. But leaving Germany has become riskier: German Jews are allowed to take less and less of their wealth and nobody wants them if they have no money. In March, Pope Pius XI promulgates a new encyclical, *Mit brennender Sorge* (With Burning Concern), denouncing Nazi neopaganism and anti-Semitism. Five days later, in another encyclical, *Divini Redemptoris,* the pope severely condemns Communism as atheist and materialist. Several days after the publication of *Mit brennender Sorge,* Cardinal George William Mundelein of Chicago speaks against Hitler, forcefully attacking Nazism. Pius XI supports the cardinal and Vatican Secretary of State Pacelli finds himself forced to placate the German ambassador to the Vatican, Diego von Bergen.

That same year a new edition of the *Protocols of the Elders of Zion* appears in Italian. The book, first published in 1903 in Saint Petersburg, purports to contain some twenty lectures, or protocols, delivered secretly in Basel during the 1897 Zionist Congress. The book supposedly reveals a vast and secret Jewish conspiracy to conquer the world; in fact, the protocols turn out to be a fabrication of the czarist secret police. Nonetheless, following the Russian Revolution, when fleeing White Russians bring them to the West, the protocols become famous and are translated into German, English, French, Polish, Hungarian, and Italian. Even the discovery that the protocols are nothing but a plagiarized and paraphrased version of a defamatory attack on Napoleon III published in Brussels in 1864 does nothing to stop the book's circulation.

In Italy the story is a little different. Published for the first time in Italian in 1921, the protocols appear in two different editions but are almost completely ignored. In 1937, though, the new edition is greeted with great interest and sells out in three months. That year, Jacques Maritain publishes his essay "The Impossible Anti-Semitism," in which he refers directly to the protocols.

Maritain urges his readers to consider that the anti-Semitism of a certain part of Catholic tradition is in conflict with Christian thought. But this argument has no effect on sales of the book. Nor does a famous article by the Jesuit priest Charles in the January 1938 issue of *Nouvelle Revue Théologique* in which he demonstrates the spuriousness of the protocols and concludes: "Of these protocols, of which they are supposed to be the guilty culprits, the Jews are only the victims, innocent victims."

A fourth Italian edition, published in 1938, under the title *The Jews of Italy,* includes a new chapter with an alphabetical list of Italy's ninety-eight hundred Jewish families.

A PICTURE TAKEN in August 1937 on Signor Stuflesser's terrace in Ortisei shows three little girls trying to hide behind some enormous crepe paper daisies. The girls are celebrating the return of their mother and father from a trip across Germany. Their parents tell of driving on marvelous new highways built by Hitler and talk about how their Astura glided along without so much as a bump. They admire the order, discipline, and cleanliness of the people, who have shown such a remarkable capacity for organization. They do not tell us about the huge banners outside Rosenheim, just beyond the Austrian border, that proclaim in large letters, "We do not want Jews."

Written in Gothic script in black on yellow, the banners made a strong impression on my brother, who had gone with my parents, but they didn't concern him, blond as he was and proud of his Italian nationality. He is ten years old. After admiring the changing of the guard at the military shrine in Munich and in awe of the martial mien of the black-clad SS men standing immobile as stone, my brother had my parents buy him a little toy helmet bearing a swastika. During a rest stop along one of the famous highways, he had his picture taken wearing the helmet and with his arm outstretched in the Nazi salute.

What is it that the Kodak's accordion body has fixed forever? An unconscious gesture or a momentary impulse? Excessive laxity on the part of our parents? An abrupt lapse into myopia? That winter when one of the many missionaries comes to visit the house, he strokes my brother's hair affectionately and, by way of paying him a compliment, says, "You look just like a little German." My brother pulls angrily at his blond forelock in a sudden change of heart.

IN OCTOBER our school life undergoes a big change. I begin first grade and my brother enters secondary school, leaving the Sisters of the Adoration, who have only elementary classes. He is to attend the Istituto Massimo, a Jesuit school in a big seventeenth-century building near the railway station. Every Saturday in all the schools of Mussolini's Italy, the program includes drill: exercises, marches, and muskets to train the boys for war. For the occasion, Mama buys him a new uniform from Zingone alla Maddalena, a Fascist uniform with khaki shorts and a black silk shirt.

Dressed in the outfit and wearing a beret and a waistcoat, my brother goes with Mama to meet Papa, who is arriving by train from Turin. They sit on a bench, happy and expectant, as the locomotive comes down the track emitting clouds of smoke beneath the great iron vaulted roof of Termini Station. Mama is probably wearing a felt hat and a light coat over a silk dress. Papa gets off the train a few cars down the platform carrying his overnight case protected by its beige cloth cover. He is tall and thin and wears a stiff collar; you can recognize him even at a distance by the gray hat he always holds aloft to signal his presence. Mama smiles festively and waves her hand in its light-colored glove as if to say, "Here we are! Over here!" As he approaches, Papa knits his brow ever so slightly and for a brief second the eyes behind his glasses focus on the boy in uniform. Then Papa puts his hat back on his head and blends in with the other passengers and the porters with suitcases slung over their shoulders. Mama stands with her hand raised, not sure whether to lower it or not. My brother waits with his chest puffed out, his beret just off to one side, according to the rules. Papa makes no gesture, gives no smile, just keeps walking straight ahead with his overnight case in his hand. Before my mother can open her mouth or my brother move a muscle, he passes them, keeping his eyes firmly fixed ahead. His gray hat is now indistinguishable from the others in the station hall. He disappears. Mama and my brother stand alone in front of the empty cars, the last puffs of steam turning to water on the rails.

I don't know what they say to each other as they come home from the station in the Astura, with Francesco behind the wheel. I don't know which is stronger, the humiliation or the sense of how ridiculous my brother's costume is. But his aversion to all the drill to come and to his black silk shirt and khaki shorts may well have been born in that brief trip home from the station, the metallic *M* on his beret glinting in the October sun.

1 9 3 8

ON MARCH 12, 1938, German troops cross the border into Austria. On the thirteenth the country is summoned to become part of the Third Reich. On the fourteenth Hitler enters Vienna in triumph, flanked by cheering crowds, as little girls in costume wave bouquets from behind the police barricades. In a plebiscite that will also be extended to the German electorate, the Austrians are now called upon to pronounce themselves in favor of the annexation, or *Anschluss,* that will transform their country into a new province of Germany. Excluded from the vote are the more than 200,000 Austrians who are officially listed as Jews. Immediately a grandiose campaign to convince the electorate gets under way and the Catholic Church is invited to play its part. On March 15 the archbishop of Vienna, Cardinal Theodor Innitzer, meets with Hitler. The exchange of views is so compelling that the cardinal sends out a circular to the various dioceses inviting them to endorse the *Anschluss;* his message urges that special attention be paid to youth associations. The cardinal's circular states that he has received assurances from the Führer "that the Church will never regret its loyalty to Greater Germany." On March 27 a collective declaration of Austria's bishops is read in every church in the country:

We joyfully acknowledge that the National Socialist Party has acted and continues to act with eminent success in the field of national and economic development as well as in the area of social policy for the Reich and the German nation, and especially for the poorest levels of the population. We are equally convinced that the National Socialist Party has staved off the threat of atheistic and destructive bolshevism.

The bishops wish to give their strongest blessing to these forward-looking policies and will instruct the faithful accordingly.

On the day of the plebiscite, needless to say, we consider it our national duty as Germans to declare our support for the German Reich and we expect that all believing Christians will understand what they must do on behalf of their nation.

On April 1 Cardinal Innitzer sends a message to Cardinal Adolf Bertram, president of the bishop's conference in Fulda, where the majority of German Catholic bishops are gathered, expressing his hope that they will align themselves with the Austrians. At the bottom of the appeal, just above his signature, he adds in his own hand, *"und heil Hitler!"*

All this enthusiasm elicits quite a reaction from Rome. On April 2 *L'Osservatore Romano,* the Vatican newspaper, announces that the declaration of the Austrian bishops was drafted and signed without approval by the Holy See. And the evening before, at eight o'clock, Vatican Radio broadcasts a program in German on the question "What is political Catholicism?" It is a sort of fireside chat, very critical of the Austrian episcopate and of Cardinal Innitzer in particular, hosted by a German Jesuit named Gustav Gundlach, an expert on the social doctrine of the Church. For obvious reasons he wishes to remain anonymous, but an informer in the Vatican transmits his name to Berlin, and at the end of May someone warns Gundlach that if he goes back to Germany he will be arrested.

Cardinal Innitzer, in the meantime, has been summoned urgently by Pius XI and he arrives in Rome by plane on April 5. The result of the meeting is a retraction in the form of a new declaration, in which the cardinal, on behalf of himself and the entire Austrian episcopate, urges the faithful to ignore the original one, because all

political directives are contrary to the faith and the freedom of conscience of Catholics. The statement also
warns that no government or political party is authorized
to use any previous statements in support of its own
position.

On April 10 the *Anschluss* receives a massive *Ja:* 99.08
percent of voters in Germany and 99.75 percent in
Austria approve it. The former Hapsburg Empire is now
a new province of the Reich, the Ostmark.

AS FOR ME, I have been attending first grade since
October. The weather is still cold. Outside in the garden
the sparrows peck at the gravel and the trees shimmer in
the north wind. My teacher is a fervent Fascist and the
first poem I learn is "On his mother's knee Benito sat
reading, Luigi Nason," in which I take the poet's name
to be part of the composition. On the cover of my notebook the king and the Duce show off their tall white
plumes. The king is short and has delicate features, as
you can see in the newsreels that I watch on Saturday
afternoons, sinking back into my seat and into deep
boredom, when Papa takes us with him to the Cinema
Planetario. The Duce, on the other hand, is stout and
muscular and rides on horseback through Villa Torlonia
or stands bare-chested in the snow with skis on his feet.

A giant-sized photograph of him reigns over the dining room of the hotel in Terminillo, a ski resort recently opened to the delight of the residents of Rome, and where we are sometimes taken to go sledding.

The only thing that makes me sad is that I don't have a "Little Italian" uniform. At home they think I don't need one; if necessary I can use my sister Teresa's. But at school the nuns never ask me to come in uniform; they say it's used only when you take the graduating exam at the end of fifth grade. I'm sorry not to have the wheel-shaped cape and the silky beret. When we play dress-up my sisters turn the cape into a long skirt that goes down to their feet, while I've got to be content with tying around my waist the big flowered handkerchief we use as a shade for the bedside lamp at night. For some reason that must go back to our infancy, our dress-up games always involve only the "front"; the behind parts—our rear ends, our backs, our calves—are not important at all.

But most of the time my sisters make use of the ironing board covers to play nun, lining our dolls, their abused pupils, up in front of them in rows of chairs. I have an instinctive aversion to dressing up in nun's clothes, even as a game, and I prefer tying the big flowered handkerchief on my head to play teacher. Sometimes I turn myself into a "sporty lady" by using a diaper pin to fasten my skirt between my legs so it looks like

I'm wearing pants. The sporty lady drives a car and knows how to pilot an airplane. She smokes and plays tennis.

FOR OVER A YEAR a press campaign has been going on to sensitize Italian public opinion to the too often neglected issue of "race." The opening blast was sounded in April 1937 by the appearance in all the bookstores of a new book by Paolo Orano, *The Jews in Italy;* which calls on Jews to reject "foreign loyalties" and their cultural heritage, and to blend in with the Fascist masses. Then the annexation of Austria seems to galvanize our Duce, who doesn't want to be left behind on the race question. Before long race is all over the national press, not only the openly anti-Semitic papers, like *Il Tevere,* Giovanni Preziosi's *La Vita Italiane,* Roberto Farinacci's magazine *Il Regime Fascista,* and Oberdan Cotone's new satirical series *Il Giornalissimo,* but the large-circulation moderate papers as well, like *Il Resto di Carlino, La Stampa, Il Messaggero,* and *Il Corriere della Sera.* There are only rare exceptions to the general chorus. One is *Il Piccolo* of Trieste, edited by Rino Alessi, but eventually Alessi is tamed and falls back into line. Emilio De Bono, one of the leaders of the 1922 Fascist march on Rome and now head of the police, is able to note in his diary entry for September 3, 1938, "The press . . . is even more disgustingly servile than usual."

The attacks on the Jews cover a vast panorama, from the Jews in finance and the stock market to the Jews in the press, in agriculture, in trade, and in the theater, from the film industry to the navy to the world of music. Even Jewish athletes are not spared. The language of this new journalism is higher in pitch and lower in style. There is, for example, this comment in the October 5, 1938, issue of *Roma Fascista* on a report of some Jews' being stopped at the border trying to leave the country with a part of their property: "No Jews, Jew lovers, or suspect persons should be allowed to leave Italy with anything more than some pocket money, their clothes, and their ugly faces. But if they should try to use their clothes to hide even so much as a five-cent piece, they should be stripped naked and pushed over the border to the tune of kicks in the rear."

Among the intellectuals, one of the favorite targets, even though he's only half Jewish, is Alberto Pincherle (who uses the pen name Alberto Moravia). But even Benedetto Croce comes under attack when his review, *La Critica,* publishes an epistolary article in defense of the Jews by the humanist Antonio Galateo. The same thing happens to Ezio Garibaldi when he joins in with a hard-hitting article in *Camicie Rosse.* A protest by the futurist poet Filippo Marinetti, who enjoys great prestige among the Fascist entourage, will provoke greater consternation. In the December 1938 issue of the journal *Artecrazia,* Marinetti will launch a violent attack against the Fascist racial laws from a cultural perspective, claiming that, as in Germany, anti-Semitism is being used as a weapon to attack modern art. The journal will be confiscated immediately but clandestine copies circulate for a long time to come.

These are still isolated cases, however. And although the majority of Italians don't respond to the new racist line with the level of enthusiasm that Mussolini might expect, the intellectuals fail to demonstrate even a shadow of the staunch opposition that more than a few people are hoping they will mount. There is instead a kind of craven assent, a desire to please so intense as to inspire Francesco Biondolillo to write in the April 14, 1939, issue of *L'Unione Sarda:* "Perhaps the worst danger comes from narrative prose that, beginning with Italo Svevo, a sly old Jew, and continuing with Alberto Moravia, an even slyer Jew, attempts to weave a great loathsome net to fish down into the slimy bottom of society for repugnant figures of men who are not men but spineless beings, muddied with base and repugnant sexuality, morally and physically sick. . . . The masters of these novelists are those specimens of pathology called Marcel Proust and James Joyce, foreign names and Jewish to the marrow of their bones, subversives to the roots of their hair." (In the postwar years Biondolillo will be authorized to teach and, besides teaching in a Roman high school, will give a number of lectures in Italian literature at l'Università La Sapienza in Rome.)

To reward such willing support and keep enthusiasm alive, the Fascist government decides to increase—up to three times its previous level—government subsidies to intellectuals.

There are a lot of writers willing to sign their names to articles whose rhetorical sails billow and strain to extoll the Italian race and bemoan the threat to its purity posed by the Jews. Many are little older than boys, educated in Fascist schools, but some of them are adults, "full-grown men," as they would have said back then. A typical example is Guido Piovene, who is thirty years old in 1938 and already a recognized intellectual, journalist, and novelist. In November, with the racial laws still hot off the presses, he agrees to review a repulsive book by Telesio Interlandi, the editor of *La Difesa della Razza* (The Defense of the Race), a new magazine that has an aggressive, unconventional graphic design and that is backed by major banks like Banca Commerciale, Credito Italiano, and Banco di Sicilia; industries like Breda and Officine Villar Perosa; and the insurance companies Riunione Adriatica di Sicurità and Istituto Nazionale delle Assicurazioni. The book is called *Contra Judeos* and in his review, published in *Il Corriere della Sera,* Piovene will write: "The first task the book promotes is to clarify for the Italian people that race is a scientific, biological fact based on an affinity of blood. The second is to demonstrate that the inferiority of some races is perpetual, that when races are mixed the inferior prevails over the superior, that the Italian race must guard its immunity.... The Jews can only be the enemies and the oppressors of any nation that takes them in. Being of different blood and conscious of their bonds, they cannot but place themselves in opposition to the alien race. The enormous number of positions of eminence occupied by the Jews in Italy is the result of a tenacious struggle. As foreigners they attempt to triumph over the other people's national culture, moving it toward 'Europeistic' forms, detaching it from the popular roots of art, as has happened in Italy."

WE CHILDREN are reading our own strange propaganda, *Euro, ragazzo aviatore* (Euro, Boy Aviator). Written by Gino Chelazzi and published in the My Children's Library series, it is the story of a young boy, "audacious and bold," who pilots a plane in a contest from which Italy must emerge victorious. A thousand perils threaten the ardent will of our hero, who with firm heart and steady pulse holds the course undaunted on his difficult flight. Euro is the young ideal of great

Fascist Italy, an Italy that can no longer tolerate the underhanded tricks of its invidious enemies. Chief among these is the Jew Jacob Manussai, "a lurid old man with a long shock of hair and a dirty white goatee, hooked nose, bushy eyebrows, sharp eyes peering out from behind a pair of glasses, flabby lips that part to reveal his yellowing fangs," who tries to foil Euro's brave enterprise—all in vain, thanks in part to Giorgione Pascal, a reformed Italian Amercian gangster.

Despite the enthusiasm that Chelazzi pours into his description of this amazing adventure, the arrogant and insolent Euro isn't much of a success with us children. Compared with the exciting adventures of *Teleferica misteriosa* (The Mysterious Cable Car) or *Torre del nord* (Tower North), we think his exploits in his seaplane are boring and stupid.

MEANWHILE, the signs of what will happen next are becoming more and more evident. Though Pius XI is far more stubborn in his opposition than anyone could have predicted, negotiations between the Vatican and Mussolini continue, under the guidance of the papal nuncio, Cardinal Francesco Borgognini-Duca. Mussolini hopes to elicit a benevolent statement from the pope by emphasizing how much the new political orientation harkens back to the Church's own centuries-old propensity with regard to the Jews, "discrimination without persecution."

But Pius XI is not a timid or malleable man and the encounter with Mussolini is very difficult. Mussolini seeks to enact a series of racial laws, and desires the pope's blessing. His objections are numerous and one in particular seems insurmountable: the provision nullifying marriages between Catholics and converted Jews (and unconverted Jews, too, for those marriages celebrated in churches). The provision is in direct violation of the 1929 Lateran Treaty between the Holy See and Mussolini, in which the state recognized the validity of all church marriages.

To Mussolini's relief, *La Civiltà Cattolica,* the official magazine of the Jesuits, which enjoys great prestige because of its ties to the Vatican secretary of state, adopts a much softer and understanding attitude toward the "Jewish question." The journal has chosen a line in favor of "a segregation or distinction suitable to our time." Signed by Father Enrico Rosa, the magazine's editor in chief from 1915 to 1931 and still one of its most authoritative editors, articles condemning biological racism nonetheless advise maintaining a certain wariness of the Jews, "not because they are of the Hebrew race but because of their attitudes and their culture."

But Pius XI has not finished causing trouble for the regime. When Hitler arrives in Rome on May 2, 1938, the whole city is lit up in celebration; only the Vatican is dark. To avoid meeting the Führer the pope has gone to Castel Gandolfo on April 30, beginning his summer vacation early. And on May 3 Pius XI publishes in *L'Osservatore Romano* a series of propositions on racism that he denounces as unacceptable, a little eight-point primer that *La Congregazione Romana* has already sent out to Catholic universities on April 13.

On the evening of Hitler's arrival, I am taken to see the Colosseum and via dell'Impero all lit up. The columns have been decorated with great bronze plates holding burning fires. I have never seen anything like it; the plates where the flames rise up, blown by the wind, are called "tripods." Hitler rules the Germans and Annemarie is proud of him. The French nuns, however, are not so fond of Hitler. When I tell Mother Gregoria about the bronze plates and the fire she screws up her little nose.

It's Sunday morning and Papa is still in bed. I've crawled in between the sheets to have him tell me the fable of the naughty goat. I love Papa's body, its fragile skinniness inside his pajamas, the pale white skin of his arms sticking out of those oversized sleeves; his way of telling a story, at once funny and instructive; his gray-blue eyes, from which the naughty goat seems to come jumping out at me. A cool clear light, almost liquid, brightens the gray buildings in front of our house, but it must not be very late because Italia knocks on the door to bring in the newspapers she bought on her way home from Mass. "There's no *Osservatore Romano,*" she says. "What do you mean? It should have been on the newsstands since yesterday afternoon," Papa says, sounding surprised. "The man at the newsstand said, 'None of those sacristy newspapers today . . .'" Italia answers, tossing a look of disdain in his direction. She remains standing in the doorway as if the gravity of the event has suddenly conferred some sort of authority on her. The little goat has disappeared from Papa's gray-blue eyes; I won't be seeing her again this morning. I don't know the meaning of the phrase "sacristy newspapers," but I share the surprise and the general disapproval of what has disturbed my idyllic Sunday morning.

A few days later it's even worse. Someone insults Italia and grabs the just-purchased *Osservatore Romano* out of her hands. This time her wide olive-skinned face is contorted from breathlessness and her hands are waving around in the air as if she's trying to defend herself from some threat, her checkered apron sticking out below the hem of her overcoat.

At the end of May, three weeks after Hitler's visit, the Office of Racial Police of the Reich discreetly installs one of its commissions in Milan to assist its Fascist colleagues.

On July 2, Father Enrico Rosa reviews for *La Civiltà Cattolica* a confutation of Nazi racism published in Switzerland by Rudolf Laemmel and entitled *The "Modern Theory of the Races" Refuted by a Non-Catholic.* Although he accepts the author's thesis with respect to atheistic German racism, Father Rosa goes on to write:

> The author exaggerates, however, too forgetful of the Jews' continuous persecution of the Christians, especially of the Catholic Church, and of the Jews' alliance with the Masons, the socialists, and other anti Christian parties; he exaggerates too when he concludes that "it would not only be illogical and antihistorical but an outright moral betrayal if Christianity today were to fail to come to the aid of the Jews." Nor can we forget that the Jews have always brought upon themselves and continue today to bring upon themselves the just aversion of peoples against their all too frequent abuses of power and their hatred of Christ himself, of his religion and his Catholic Church, almost taking up the cries of their forefathers who cursed the blood of the Just and the Holy.

IN JULY, while we children are running through the fields of Ortisei as we do every summer, a sizable number of university professors and their assistants offer the Duce the gift he most desires, the official seal of approval of science, a kind of intellectual ratification of his campaign for the protection of the Roman-Italic race. On July 25 (a date that five years later will mark Mussolini's fall from power), a press release from the National Fascist Party reveals the names of the illustrious drafters of the "Manifesto of the Racial Scientists," published anonymously on July 14 in *Il Giornale d'Italia*. The document is actually called "Il fascismo e i problemi della razza" (Fascism and the Race Question) and was drafted by Guido Landra, a young assistant professor of anthropology, under the guidance of Mussolini and Dino Alfieri, the Italian ambassador to the Vatican. It is presented to the public, however, as the work of the eminent director of the Rome Institute of Medical Pathology, Professor Nicola Pende (he will hold on to his position until 1955), a scholar of international stature and senator of the realm, in collaboration with the distinguished Arturo Donaggio, professor of neuropsychiatry in Modera (he will die in 1942); Franco Savorgnan, professor of statistics in Rome and president of the Central Bureau of Statistics (he will remain in his position until 1949); Sabato Visco, professor of general physiology and director of the National Nutrition Institute in Rome (he will retain his position until 1963); and Edoardo Zavattari, professor of zoology in Rome (until 1958). These professors are joined by a number of assistants: Lino Businco, Lidio Cipriani, Leone Franzi, the above-mentioned Guido Landra, and

Marcello Ricci. With the manifesto's findings, Mussolini is able to officially declare that the orientation of the Italian race is Nordic Aryan.

The "Manifesto" explains to the forty-four million Italians the existence of races, their different characteristics, and finally the importance of the race they themselves (excluding the 48,032 Jews) belong to and the necessity of keeping such a heritage genetically pure to maintain the characteristics that have distinguished it throughout the world. This "scientific" explanation is used to validate the destruction of two great Italian institutes of learning, the Institute of Physics and the Institute of Mathematics. Racism and cultural nihilism will descend on them like an ax, decimating their prestigious faculties. The Institute of Mathematics will sink into a period of isolation that will remove it forever from the position of international prestige held since the beginning of the century. The four-line dismissal letter signed by Institute Chancellor Cardinali reads: "Your personal records show that you belong to the Hebrew race. You have therefore been suspended from service beginning October 16, 1938 XVI, in accordance with Royal Decree Law 5-9-1938 No. 1390." The letter ends the careers of seven prominent mathematicians: Tullio Levi Civita, a member of the French Academy of Sciences and the only Italian editor of the prestigious German journal *Zenterblatt für Mathematik* (whose top editors will resign in protest over his dismissal); Federico Enriques, Corrado Segré, and Guido Castelnuovo, founders of the Italian school of algebraic geometry; Guido Fubini, Guido Ascoli, Gino Fano, and Alessandro Terracini. And this is only a partial list. For the Institute of Physics, the expulsions of Emilio Segré, Eugenio Fubini, Leo Pincherle, Bruno Rossi, and Enrico Fermi, who will join the others because his wife is Jewish, will mean the end of that extraordinary experience that is known as the School of Via Panisperna. Six years later David Hilbert, one of the world's leading mathematicians, will be asked by the Reich minister of culture at a banquet at the University of Göttingen if the Italian Institute of Mathematics had suffered because of the expulsion of the Jews. "Suffered?" replied Hilbert. "No, it didn't suffer, Mr. Minister, it simply doesn't exist anymore."

Listing all those suspended from the various disciplines would take many more pages. To keep these professors of inferior race from sullying the good name of Italy abroad, they are also prohibited from participating in any international conferences.

When Levi Civita dies in 1941, tended not even by a nurse (since Jews will be barred from hiring Aryan domestic help), the only newspaper to remember him with an obituary will be *L'Osservatore Romano*. Levi

Civita was also a member of the Papal Academy of Science.

But there is no doubt that it is the academy's own teaching faculties that gives Mussolini his greatest satisfaction. Among the full-time and adjunct senior faculty there are some 98 Jewish professors and another 194 Jewish members of the junior faculty—almost three hundred jobs that laws prohibiting non-Aryan appointments render immediately vacant, making it much easier for the rest of the faculty to digest measures that otherwise might have seemed indigestible. The bitter pill is made even sweeter by the fact that many of the newly vacant posts now up for grabs are among the most prestigious of chaired and tenured positions. The only real worry expressed by the remaining faculty involves positions that cannot be filled immediately; hurried and ever more pressing appeals are made requesting that temporarily vacant posts not be eliminated and that each university department be allowed to maintain its share of faculty positions. Among those named to fill the vacant posts, only one, Massimo Bontempelli, refuses to take over a tenured position forcibly abandoned by a teacher of the "Hebrew race."

Just about the same time as the "Manifesto of the Racial Scientists" is published, the minister of internal affairs announces that the Central Bureau of Statistics has been transformed into the General Office of Demography and Race. Over the next five years, this new creation, called Demorazza for short, will decide the fates of tens of thousands of Italian and foreign Jews, backed by a ruthless Race Tribunal that will rule on appeals filed by those trying to find a loophole in the net of racial discrimination.

ON JULY 16, in its page 2 report on the publication of the "Manifesto," *L'Osservatore Romano* limits itself to a brief summary, highlighting the "'objective scientific findings,' whose aims are different from those commonly associated with 'racism' and which appear to give more weight to 'spiritual' rather than 'biological' differences, insofar as there are no superior or inferior races." Also on July 16, in *La Civiltà Cattolica,* a Father Barbera comments favorably on the anti-Semitic measures approved by the Hungarian government, which has imposed quotas on the number of Jews in public life and the professions.

But although the "Manifesto" doesn't seem to upset the upper ecclesiastical ranks in that it "discriminates but does not persecute," it provokes a decidedly negative reaction from Pius XI. On July 15, during an audience granted to the mother superiors of the Society of Our Lady of the Cenacle, the pope delivers a wide-ranging and detailed refutation of what he calls "exaggerated nationalism," declaring:

> it hinders the healthy growth of the soul and raises barriers between peoples. It is contrary not only to the law of God but to the faith itself, to the Credo itself, to that Credo that is sung in all the cathedrals of the world. . . . "Catholic" means "universal"; there is no other possible translation, either in Italian or in any other modern language.

And just a few days later, speaking to 150 young ecclesiastical assistants from Catholic Action, a nonpolitical advocacy movement, the pope returns to the same theme:

> Unfortunately there is something much worse than any of the various formulas of racism or nationalism, and that is the spirit that lies behind them. It must be said that there is something particularly detestable about this spirit of separatism, this exaggerated nationalism, which precisely because it is un-Christian, irreligious, becomes in the end inhuman.

In his famous speech of July 28 to the students of the Institute for the Propagation of the Faith, Pius XI asks himself "why in the world Italy, so unhappily, felt the need to imitate Germany" and goes on to affirm that "there is only one human race," stressing that racism is foreign to Italian tradition.

When Mussolini learns of this last speech (characterized by Galeazzo Ciano, Mussolini's son-in-law and foreign minister, in his diary entry for July 30, as "violently antiracist"), he orders the press to ignore it. And the local police prefects are sent a circular telling them to block its publication in parish newsletters. The papal nunico, Cardinal Borgognini-Duca, however, tries to make peace. After a meeting on July 30 in which Ciano informs him of the Duce's irritation over Pius XI's public statements, Ciano is able to write that "the nuncio . . . showed himself personally to be quite anti-Semitic."

The next day the newspapers report Mussolini's response to the pope, delivered during a visit to a Fascist young officers' camp: "You must know, and everyone must know, that with respect to the issue of race, we are going to hold our course. To say that Fascism has imitated someone or something else is simply absurd."

L'Osservatore Romano fails to give a full report of Pius XI's speech to the students of the Institute for the Propagation of the Faith. Does this reflect a decision made in his supervisory capacity by the Vatican's secretary of state, Cardinal Pacelli? Or did Pius XI himself suddenly decide to tread cautiously? The latter hypothesis seems less likely. Indeed, on September 6, speaking to a group of pilgrims from Belgian Catholic Radio, Pius XI reiterates, in even more unequivocal terms, his condemnation of "separatist nationalism" and "racism."

This pronouncement, however, is something of a mystery. The pilgrims are led by Monsignor Picard, president of Belgian Catholic Radio. In Picard's story of the encounter, published in three different newspapers— *La Croix, La Documentation Catholique,* and *La Libre Belgique*—the pope's speech, at his express request, is reported in full. Monsignor Picard recounts that, before the speech, he and two other pilgrims were received by the pope and presented him with a missal. The other pilgrims were then received and the pope, leafing through the missal, paused for a moment over the Canon of the Mass: *"Supra quae propitio ac sereno vultu habere dignatus es pueri tui justi Abel, et sacrificum Patriarchae nostri Abrahamae."* Here the pope stopped reading, turned to Monsignor Picard, and commented:

Abel's sacrifice, Abraham's sacrifice . . . the whole religious history of humanity in just three lines . . . A glorious passage. Whenever I read the words, "The sacrifice of our father Abraham," I cannot help being deeply moved. Mark well, we call Abraham our patriarch, our ancestor. Anti-Semitism is not compatible with the idea . . . expressed in this passage. It is an antithetical movement that we Christians have nothing to do with.

At this point, according to Monsignor Picard, the pope could no longer contain himself and, his voice breaking, he quoted a line from Saint Paul highlighting our spiritual descent from Abraham. "No," he concluded, "it is not possible for Christians to take part in anti-Semitism. . . . Spiritually, we are Semites."

L'Osservatore Romano reports the encounter as having taken place on two different days, September 6 and 7. On the sixth, according to the Vatican newspaper, three people were received, including Monsignor Picard, and they presented the pope with a *radio*. The same day, according to *L'Osservatore Romano,* the pope granted an audience to four hundred members of Catholic Action. The paper does not report the pope's speech to this second group but comments on it at length, emphasizing that the pope wanted above all to counsel against debating the question of anti-Semitism in terms of racism because it could too easily lead to misunderstanding. The meeting with the pilgrims from Belgian Catholic Radio, on the other hand, supposedly took place on the seventh, and in its account of the pope's speech the Vatican newspaper leaves out some passages, including the ones cited above.

ON SEPTEMBER 18 Mussolini is in Trieste to commemorate Italy's victory in World War I. Warships are at anchor in the harbor and the sea shines brightly between the deep green banks of the gulf; the festive overflow crowd spills out of the square into the nearby side streets. The Duce is elated over the Blackshirts' successes in the Spanish civil war and he launches himself into the subject that seems to be closest to his heart. "With regard to domestic policy, the most pressing problem we now face is the racial question," he declares, biting off the syllables one by one.

> Because history teaches us that empires are won with arms but are held with prestige. And achieving prestige depends on having a clear, rigorous racial consciousness that knows how to recognize not only differences but also clear superiorities. . . . Nevertheless, Jews of Italian citizenship who have demonstrated unquestionable military or civil distinction on behalf of Italy and the regime will be treated with understanding and fairness. As for the others, we will implement a policy of separation . . .

He continues: "In the end the world will be surprised more by our generosity than by our severity. Unless"—and here his tone becomes threatening—"unless Semites from beyond our borders, and those within them, and above all their unexpected and newfound friends who defend them from too many pulpits"—the allusion to

Pius XI could not be more explicit and the voice hangs suspended for a split second as the crowd explodes in an ovation of consensus—"should force us into a radical change of direction." Less than a month later, during the October 6 meeting of the Fascist Grand Council where the racial laws will be approved by a large majority, he will be even more imperious: "I declare this pope injurious to the fate of the Catholic Church."

The Grand Council's meeting goes from ten o'clock in the evening to three in the morning and ends in the agreement of all except Emilio De Bono, Luigi Feder-zoni, and Italo Balbo, who expresses his opposition with his usual vehemence. The debate is quite heated. (Balbo will die in 1940, in the early days of the war, during a reconnaissance flight; the precise circumstances of his death will remain a mystery forever.)

IT IS AUTUMN in Rome. The final days of October fade softly into a light of ruddy red leaves and sudden rain. A last-minute agreement between Mussolini and the Holy See allows Catholic schools to accept Jewish students who practice the Catholic religion. But for mixed marriages it's still war, and on November 4 Pius XI writes a letter to the king declaring that the new provisions on matrimony are a violation of the Lateran

Treaty. On November 5 he writes to Mussolini on the same subject. The king responds only that he has forwarded the pope's letter to the Duce, without further comment. Mussolini doesn't respond at all but lets it be known that he "has the impression the Vatican is pulling too tightly on the rope." In his diary entry for the sixth, Foreign Minister Ciano writes, "Storm on the horizon with the Church." On November 13, three days after ratification of the racial laws by the Council of Ministers, the Holy See, through papal nuncio Borgognini-Duca, presents an official letter of protest to the Italian embassy for violation of article 34 of the treaty. On November 15 Ciano notes in his diary, "Protest, actually very bland, sent by the Holy See . . ."

The pope's position, in fact, is not shared by the entire College of Cardinals, and the issue of mixed marriages is glossed over by a series of more or less veiled concessions made by both sides but mostly by the Church. An open conflict with Pius XI having been averted for the moment, the new laws are ready to be published and promulgated. What is so important anyway about 48,032 "persons," as they will be referred to from now on in official documents.

In the fall of 1938 there are 58,412 Jewish residents in Italy, but 10,380 of them are foreigners and only 48,032 are Italians: that's how many are recorded by the census conducted by the Demorazza office (and the census lists in police headquarters around the country will prove to be very helpful to Theodor Dannecker's SS, which after September 8, 1943, will be in charge of rounding the Jews up and deporting them). In a population of 44 million, they represent about one-tenth of 1 percent. If we consider only the 37,241 who are registered as members of the Jewish community, the percentage is even smaller. They are a tiny minority who are perfectly integrated into the social life of the country's large and small cities, mostly in the north and central regions, and who, once freed from the restrictions that limited their freedom before Italy was unified in 1870, have been successful in commerce and in the professions. There are no rural Jewish communities and there is really no significant Jewish presence in high finance.

In Rome the first Jewish settlements go back to the pre-Christian era, and the ghetto, situated between the Tiber and Octavian's Arch, where until the unification of Italy the gates were locked at night, is populated primarily by families who make their living in the retail trade. With the exception of a few deep, dusty, labyrinthine stores, most of their businesses are small shops that have built up a clientele over the years by offering good quality and fair prices. And whether they are intellectuals or shopkeepers, professionals or businessmen, whether they live in Rome or scattered up and down the

peninsula, almost all the Jews have tried to demonstrate
their patriotism by fighting in the First World War or by
serving as officials in the public administration. They
have participated actively in politics. A fair number are
even supporters of Fascism. They have never engaged in
proselytizing, because their religion does not require it,
and, unlike Jews in some other countries, few of them
know Hebrew other than religious texts and they speak
not Yiddish but local Italian dialects. Their religious cer-
emonies, whose rituals have been handed down for centuries, are conducted with great discretion so as not to
attract the attention or the alarm of the Church, ever
vigilant and suspicious of those who "obstinately refuse
to convert." During the Holy Week liturgy of the Passion
of Christ, the members of the apostolic Roman Church
stand amid the purple drapes that darken their churches
and recite out loud that the Jewish people chose to sacrifice the Redeemer rather than save him by putting
Barabbas, an assassin, in his place.

THE ROYAL DECREE: Laws on Race are published on November 19, effective immediately. The first
of the decrees establishes the criteria for belonging to
the Aryan race and the measures to be adopted with
respect to non-Aryans (meaning Jews). The following
people are declared to be Jews: those with two Jewish

parents, even if they themselves practice a different religion; those with one Jewish and one foreign parent; those with only one Jewish parent who practice the Jewish religion. Membership in the Jewish race must be declared and recorded in the registry of births, deaths, and marriages.

The decree also defines subcategories of the Jewish race whose members will be exempt from the laws because of exceptional merit: families of those killed in combat; of those who enlisted in the armed forces during war; of those decorated for wartime service; of those who died in defense of Fascism; of Fascists enrolled during the years 1919–22 and during the second half of 1924; of veterans of the opening shot of the Fascist revolution, the 1919 occupation of Fiume.

According to the provisional results of a secret census, some 3,502 families are eligible for the exemption. (There will, however, be 8,171 applications for exemptions, of which, between 1938 and 1943, 5,870 will be reviewed and, despite increasingly rigid standards of review, 2,486 will be granted, for a total of 6,994 people.)

The list of prohibitions for "persons declared to be of Jewish race" is long. An initial series pertains to education and culture in general. Teaching in any grade and at any school attended by Italian students is prohibited. Membership in academies, institutes, or associations of science, arts, or letters is prohibited. Enrollment and attendance in any grade and at any school attended by Italian students is prohibited. A transitional provision allows Jewish students already enrolled in universities to finish their degrees, but only if they are not, now or in the future, behind in their studies.

A second series of prohibitions have as their first objective the purity of the party. Membership in the National Fascist Party is prohibited. The army is only fourth on the list: military service is prohibited during peace or war. Then comes property: ownership or management of companies involved in the defense of the nation or of companies with more than a hundred workers is prohibited. Ownership of land whose value is greater than five thousand lire or of urban buildings whose overall value is greater than twenty thousand lire is prohibited. Lastly, the employment of domestic servants of Italian race is prohibited.

The last decree is a kind of summa of all those leading up to it. Jews are to be excluded from the civil and military administration of the state; from the administrations of provinces, cities, and public bodies; from institutions and agencies, including public transportation and municipal agencies; from state-related entities, from banks of national interest, and from private insurance companies.

Additional provisions prohibit any school from adopting textbooks by Jewish authors; books by more than one author are likewise prohibited if any of the authors is Jewish. Later on a further series of measures will add the final touch, prohibiting Jews from going to vacation resorts, from staying in hotels, from placing advertisements or obituaries in newspapers, from owning radios with more than five valves, from publishing books, from writing for the press under a pseudonym, from giving lectures, and from listing their names in the telephone book.

For all practical purposes, 48,032 Italians of the Jewish religion or from Jewish families who in the month of October were still full citizens with all their civil rights intact now find themselves in November transformed into "persons of the Jewish race," and as such, besides being recorded on a separate list, they are deprived of the status enjoyed by the rest of their fellow Italians and finally are stripped of most of their private property. For many, the majority, the laws will also mean the loss of their jobs, and for all of them eventually the loss of the right to study.

Isolated from the rest of the population, these 48,000 "persons" find themselves from one day to the next at the mercy of their former fellow citizens, who not infrequently will give in to the temptation to take advantage of the situation. In the space of one month, through no fault of their own, the Jews have become bargaining chips in negotiations with the country's glorious German ally.

Next the Jews will be asked to leave Italy. To implement this policy a new decree is drawn up that allows Jews leaving in the first year to take with them 80 percent of their property. But after the fifth year, if they still haven't left, they will be allowed to take only 30 percent. And if they insist on staying after that they will have to pay a surtax of 10 percent in the first year and on up to 100 percent in the fifth year. Then their remaining property will be confiscated and they will be expelled and interned in work camps.

For economic reasons, these provisions will never be put into practice—it is too burdensome in a crucial year like 1939 to give up even a small part of the national wealth—and besides, how can you expatriate if you don't have a passport? Passports will be reissued to younger Jews for a short time, and those with the necessary initiative and courage—ready to start from scratch without a penny to their names—will leave, as will those few who, gifted with greater foresight, have already transferred a part of their holdings abroad. Later on, with the outbreak of the war, expatriation will become almost impossible due to the considerable if not total lack of willingness of foreign countries to accept refugees unable to support themselves and to the ever more restrictive measures introduced by the Italian Office of Public Safety.

AS AN IMMEDIATE CONSEQUENCE of the racial decrees, the Treves family of Milan, owners since 1861 of a publishing house that has published works by Verga, D'Annunzio, and Pirandello and that now publishes the magazine *L'Illustrazione Italiana,* are forced to sell the business. It is bought by the industrialist Aldo Garzanti, who holds the Italian franchise for chemical products made by Du Pont de Nemours.

In Florence, the publisher Bemporad is also forced to sell. An important name in scholarly publishing, Bemporad's catalog includes the works of Dante as well as the most important authors of the twentieth century.

The case of the publisher Formìggini of Modena is a somewhat more dramatic example. Formìggini belongs to a Jewish family that has been in Italy for over three hundred years and that, because of its commercial and cultural prestige, has had a papal dispensation from the limitations placed on Jews living in the Papal States. Along with many other works, Angelo Fortunato Formìggini is the publisher of *Classics for Fun* and of *Apologie,* texts about the various religions that have been translated into a number of languages. In 1918 he founded the Istituto Leonardo for the dissemination of

Italian culture, and in 1928 he was the first to have the idea of publishing the Italian *Chi è,* modeled on the American *Who's Who.* And in the Palazzo Doria in Rome Formìggini established a library with some thirty thousand volumes. On November 29, after a futile attempt to obtain an exemption from the legislation that deprives him from one day to the next of everything he has so passionately created, he kills himself, jumping off the Ghirlandina Tower in Modena. He is sixty years old.

In a letter to his wife he explains what has brought him to this extreme gesture, which will "demonstrate the malicious absurdity of the racial provisions." He is powerless in the face of laws issued by obsequious and ignorant party hacks backed by a select group of scholars servile to the point of repudiating even the slightest notion of professional ethics. To say nothing of His Majesty Victor Emanuel III, king of Italy and emperor of Ethiopia, whose signature is affixed at the bottom of the last page of the decrees.

THE FOLLOWING YEAR, on June 29, a new decree will prohibit Jews from practicing as notaries or working as journalists. And as for Jewish physicians, pharmacists, veterinarians, obstetricians, attorneys, accountants, architects, chemists, agronomists, surveyors, and engineers, their names will be erased from the rolls of their professional associations and organizations and they will be prohibited from taking "Aryan" patients and clients. They will be permitted to practice only among themselves. All other forms of association or collaboration between Jews and Aryans will also be prohibited.

The new Civil Code will also conform to the new racial policy, decreeing in article 1: "Legal capacity shall be acquired at birth. The limitations on legal capacity deriving from membership in certain races shall be established by special laws." On July 13, Law 1024 will finally provide a definition of *Aryanized,* a term to be applied to those whom the Race Tribunal, upon request of the minister of internal affairs, shall recognize as "not belonging to the Jewish race," notwithstanding entries to the contrary in the register of births, marriages, and deaths. It is a law that is nothing if not totally arbitrary. Grotesque and tragic at the same time, it will work to the advantage of a small group of corrupt bureaucrats. "Aryanization" will eventually achieve a market value in Rome of anywhere from 500,000 to 2,000,000 lire.

The day after publication of the law excluding students of the Jewish race from public schools, the literature teacher at the Istituto Massimo, where my brother is in his second year, publicly congratulates Mario Farinacci, nephew of the more famous Roberto, who is one of the staunchest supporters of the new provisions. It doesn't seem to worry Professor Giordano that in his class there are two students of the Jewish race who are among the first victims of the new laws—two *Volljuden,* freshly converted.

WHILE JEWS in Italy are losing their rights to work, the Jews of Germany and Austria are suffering the terrors of Kristallnacht.

The German Church does not issue a formal protest. The only authoritative voice raised in defense of the persecuted is that of the vicar general of Saint Hedwig's Cathedral in Berlin, Bernhard Lichtenberg. Speaking from the pulpit on the evening of November 10, he invites his parishioners to pray for the Jews and warns them: "We know what happened yesterday. We don't know yet what will happen tomorrow but we are witnesses to what is happening today: right next door to us the synagogue is in flames, and it is a house of God just like this one."

In London the archbishop of Westminster asks the pope to show his support for a meeting seeking assistance for victims of racial and religious persecution and invites him to join in a public declaration affirming that for Christ there is no discrimination between races and that the great human family must remain united. When the invitation arrives in Rome, Vatican Secretary of State Pacelli notes, "If the thing were essentially of a private nature it would be easier, but we must avoid giving the impression of being afraid of that which one must not fear." The response drafted to decline the invitation is a small masterpiece of diplomacy:

The Holy Father has so many preoccupations at the moment, not only for his health but also for the many questions he is called upon to address, that not being able to see personally to the message requested, charges His Eminence to consider himself capable of interpreting his august thought, affirming that the Roman pontificate views with a humane and Christian eye all works of charity and assistance on behalf of those who are unjustly afflicted with pain and suffering.

Less than two months later Father Agostino Gemelli, chancellor of the Catholic University of Milan and editor in chief of the journal *Vita e Pensiero,* is invited by the University of Bologna to speak in commemoration of Guglielmo da Saliceto, the thirteenth-century physician and cleric. It is January 9, 1939, and in front of an attentive audience of students and professors, he expresses his thoughts on the Jews. "It is tragic, without doubt, and painful," he says,

to see the situation of those who cannot be part, because of their blood and their religion, of this magnificent fatherland—a tragic situation in which we see being carried out yet again, as so many times before over the centuries, that terrible sentence which the deicide people have called down upon themselves and for which they continue to wander throughout the world, unable to find the peace of a homeland, as the consequences of their horrible crime follow them everywhere and for all time.

Father Gemelli, whose name has been given to the square in front of the Catholic University of Milan as well as to a Catholic hospital in Rome, is not new to this kind of discourse. In 1924, in the pages of *Vita e Pensiero,* he commented on the recent death of Felice Momigliano:

A Jew, a high school teacher, a great philosopher, a great socialist, Felice Momigliano has died a suicide. Some spineless journalists have written equivocating, tearful obituaries. It has been mentioned that he was chancellor of the Università Mazziniana. . . . But if, together with Positivism, Socialism, Free Thought, and Momigliano, death were also to come for all those Jews who are carrying on the work of the Jews who crucified Our Lord, would not the world be better off? And would not it be an even more complete liberation if, before dying, they were to repent and ask for the water of baptism?

On January 19, 1939, Cardinal Piazza publishes a long commentary on the killing of Christ in *L'Osservatore Romano*. The Church, he observes, has had to "defend itself and its faithful from dangerous contacts with the Jews and from their invasiveness." His readers learn that "invasiveness" is "the well-known hereditary characteristic of this people."

1 9 3 9

MY DAYS haven't changed at all. The blue furniture in my room, the picture of children skating, the carousel-shaped wooden lamp haven't gathered even one more speck of dust. And although Dr. Luzzatti has been prohibited from laying his hairy ear on my feverish back, I have the soft, warm, slightly oily ear of Dr. Vannuttelli to listen to my lungs and decide whether I need to have linseed oil rubbed on my chest. Italia passes the buffer over the parquet floors and if I climb on it she takes me for a ride, gliding up and down the room. Then she says, "That's enough, get down now. You're too heavy." In the afternoons I go out with Annemarie and she takes me to play in the park along the Tiber in front of the Ministry of the Navy. She puts her coat on over her apron and when she bends down to wrap my scarf around my neck

I can smell the chicken on her skin. I like it. Letizia, the cook, on the other hand, I don't like at all. She's missing some of her front teeth and her toenails are crooked and green. Papa says she may be dirty but she's a good worker and she once made thirteen fruit pies in a single day. The boy who delivers the ice comes every morning with a big block wrapped in a jute sack and he splits it right in front of Letizia, who puts it in the wooden icebox lined with zinc. We are told nothing about the new laws that signal catastrophe for almost fifty thousand Jews—not even on Sunday night when Uncle Nino comes to dinner and we're allowed to sit at the table with the adults. Uncle Nino is a magistrate and Italia calls him Your Excellency. He is my godfather and he held me in his arms at my baptism at Saint Peter's together with Signora Basile, even though he likes only women who are pretty and cheerful like Mama.

I don't know what goes on in the apartment across the street, where every once in a while I get a glance of the newborn baby, who is now a chubby little ball sticking his head out between the columns of the railing on the balcony. And now that I'm in elementary school Annemarie doesn't take me to Villa Giulia anymore, so I don't know anything about the girl with the gold star, whether she still wears *petit bateau* underpants or still plays with her pretty colored shovel.

Nothing in that winter of 1939 disturbs the orderly course of life in via Flaminia, where the druggist and the baker have Italian names like Garibaldi and Cantiani. Nor during the following spring, when I lean out over the balcony to see the tram coming around the corner on its way to the stadium with the festive "Young Italian" girls looking out the windows, all in white and black. I envy those "little swallows," as our teacher calls them in her emphatic voice. Some terrible things will happen to make me go back and visit that time, to look down into the well that Signora Della Seta, the Levis, and the little boy across the road are sliding into with not the slightest sound. I haven't noticed that Giorgio Levi has stopped ringing our bell to go play football with my brother, although I do hear the interminable exercises that he plays every afternoon on his piano. His father, who was a high-level manager at the electric company, has lost his job and gets by translating engineering texts from English to Italian. Every now and then some friend commissions him to sell a nineteenth-century Neapolitan painting; he is believed to be an expert on such art. I ride up with him in the elevator. He's a tall, thin man and a painting, wrapped in paper and tied with a string, hangs down from one hand. He wears a hat and I can't tell if it's true that he's bald like Italia says. He lost his hair, Italia says, because of the helmet and all the sweat during the war with Libya.

. . .

NOTHING DISTURBS the orderly course of life until the screaming in the foyer, a fight over the elevator. Elsa, the concierge's wife, has just come out of the door at the foot of the stairs and she's screaming. Her husband, Domenico, isn't there and his office is empty. Elsa's deep blue eyes are fierce, and she's still drying her hands, wet from the laundry, on her apron. I've never heard her yell like this; her voice is shrill and aggressive. Giorgio Levi has just come in from outside, carrying his bicycle, and he's standing on the landing waiting for the elevator. She screams at him that he mustn't put the bicycle in the elevator, or in the concierge's office, or anywhere else for that matter, and screams again that it would be better if he didn't use the elevator at all, first because he has no right to use it and then because he always gets it muddy. Without saying a word the boy picks up the bicycle and starts to struggle up the stairs. I can see his curly hair and his knickers. Elsa follows him with her eyes until he's out of sight and only then does she go back, reassured, into the cavelike darkness of her apartment with its basement-level windows. Even if she's only a concierge, she's still an Aryan, and that kid is a "miserable Jew."

Italia and I have been standing motionless on the landing, and as soon as the elevator arrives I slip inside. I wait anxiously for Italia to close the door and push the button

for our floor, the second. And as she unbuttons my overcoat with her face right next to mine, her chicken smell
has never been so comforting, the sight of her pale,
porous skin never so reassuring. The whining creak of
the elevator is a balm that drives the fear away, sticks it
onto the shoulder of "that Levi boy," and as the door
clicks shut behind us it traps the fear inside, together with
the bicycle carried up the stairs, step by step.

That evening at home when we talk about what happened, Papa is indignant. He bitterly disapproves of
Elsa and sympathizes with the Levis, "very good people,
even though they're Jewish," forced to put up with
abuse. Instead of the zealous guardian of our safety, Elsa
now seems to have become an informer, spying on us
from her cave and recording every word, every gesture.
Papa's indignation spills over onto the stalwart Fascist
tenants on the top floor, "that kid in his black shirt who
has got to be an informer for OVRA," the political
police. And to my shocked surprise he even criticizes the
king, whom he calls "an unscrupulous lout."

But during the night I am overcome by doubt that
turns my stomach inside out: if newborn babies arrive in
baskets outside the door, who can assure me that I was
left outside the right door, that I wasn't meant for the
Della Setas? The Della Setas who are Jewish even though
they're very good people? How can I be sure, really sure,
that there wasn't some mistake and it wasn't just by error

that I was left in front of the door with the slightly rounded brass plate and Papa's name shining on it that Italia polishes every Saturday afternoon?

THE LAY SISTER pulls the weeds from around the strawberry plants and cries. The leaves on the passion-flower vines tremble in the cold. Pius XI is dead and we are looking toward Saint Peter's. The north wind lifts Mother Gregoria's veil, uncovering the short black hairs on the back of her neck. She has round, frightened eyes. The pope passed away at dawn, without a cry, without a message, as if he had been swallowed up by water, and the nuns are forlorn, waiting for a sign from heaven. They are praying, kneeling in the light wood pews of the chapel, pierced hearts pinned to their chests, their starched bonnets framing their tear-lined faces like a monstrance round the host. Long, threatening clouds unravel in the sky. Death moves on those clouds and not even the Madonna of Lourdes, enclosed in a trembling circle of candles, can stop it. We have to pray too, and when dusk sets in, as we wait to go back to our homes, we stand in silence in front of the great glass window, looking down on the valley below. The little train from the North Rome station cuts across the fallow fields where the Aniene River winds and winds back again, silver-gray between its pallid banks of cane.

But the Salve Reginas and the Ave Marias, the mournful verses of the psalms cannot bring Pius XI back to life, his hands folded on his ermine-bordered purple cape, his face like marble, his feet spread open in his white satin shoes that wiggle ever so slightly when he is placed on the bier.

In the wind that drags the clouds beyond the Soratte, strange voices move through the sky like a shudder, words barely whispered with devout trepidation, with a slight shake of the head—almost a reprimand for the Angel of Death, who swooped down like lightening just a day before the pope's speech to the bishops on the eve of the tenth anniversary of the Lateran Treaty. Tears stream down Mother Cecilia's cheeks, moistening her handkerchief. "Cardiopatia"—heart disease—she says with that liquid round French *r,* and the word bristles with pointed interrogatives as her hand points to her chest where the evil nests, to that pierced heart all aglow with red against the embroidered stain.

THERE WILL be a lot of speculation about Pius XI's undelivered speech. The only thing that's certain is the presence of some sheets of paper on his table on the night of February 10 and their disappearance the next morning. They will not reappear until 1959, when the newly elected Pope John XXIII will publish the contents of some notes. Written by a hand about to be overcome with exhaustion, the last words become inde-cipherable, like a path dissolving into the forest. It was to have been an important occasion. For the first time since he became pope in 1922, Pius XI had summoned all his bishops together. We cannot guess what words he would have chosen to denounce the abomination that was destroying not just innocent people but all sense of Christian compassion. The few notes to reemerge after twenty years seem primarily to be about seminaries and the education of the clergy, and only the last paragraph addresses, in a much more dramatic tone, the most burn-ing theme:

> The press is capable of saying anything against Us and against the things most dear to Us, even to the point of recalling in false and perverse interpretations the recent and ancient history of the Church, down to the pertinacious denial of any persecution in Ger-many, a denial accompanied by false and slanderous accusations of political interference . . .

Then the writing becomes illegible, the syllables dis-torted, the hand no longer able to hold the pen.

The last words to reach us were those pronounced in a speech to the cardinals on Christmas Eve 1938, when Pius XI called the swastika "the enemy of the cross of

Christ." The next morning, on our knees in front of the radio, Mama and Papa, Letizia, Italia, Annemarie, and we children had listened in silence as he delivered the papal blessing *urbi et orbi* to the city of Rome and to the world. His voice was still steady despite his age, clear and very near, the syllables enunciated one by one as if the Latin formula had to express the prophecy of the sibyl.

He was a pope not easily intimidated, a tough nut to crack for those who have decided to join forces with the murderer in the ankle-length overcoat, the man with the hate-filled voice. In his last audience, granted to Prime Minister Neville Chamberlain and Lord Halifax of England, Pius XI had once again clearly expressed what he thought about reactionary regimes and the duties of democracy, about racial persecution and the urgent need to come to the aid of the refugees. Pointing to the portraits of Thomas More and Cardinal Fisher, he added, "I sit here and think of the English and it pleases me to think that these men represented the best to their people—their courage, their decisiveness, their readiness to fight, to die if necessary, for what they believed was right."

It seems quite strange to find among the names of the physicians responsible for the pope's health on that morning of February 10, 1939, that of Marcello Petacci, brother of the more famous Claretta, who occupies a special place in the heart of our Duce. The Petacci family has been making a name for itself for some time now, and thanks to the privileges its members enjoy, they've been able to build themselves a Hollywood-style villa on the slopes of Monte Mario in the green suburbs of Rome, where Mussolini has his home. But this doesn't mean anything—Pius XI was eighty-two years old, a venerable age, and the day chosen for his speech to the bishops was also the seventeenth anniversary of his coronation. And so at 4:30 a.m. when Vatican Radio suddenly announced to the world that the pope had been taken ill, no one was all that surprised. Actually, Pius XI had already died, but it wasn't until 5:15, as the dawn brushed its colors on the contours of a city still immersed in sleep, that a voice without intonation, grave, slow, well suited to the solemnity of the event, gave the news: Pius XI is no longer of this world. As the first trolley cars rattled down the tracks on their way out of the depot and the milkmen loaded up their metal baskets with freshly filled glass bottles, noisily breaking the truce of sleep, the pope's term had ended.

Two months before, on December 14, when the tension with Pius XI was at its greatest point, Mussolini had made no secret of his intolerance to his son-in-law Ciano (who had diligently recorded in his diary, "I reported to the Duce on my conversation with Pignatti [Italy's ambassador to the Vatican]. He exploded with anger at the pope, who he hopes will die soon.") Now when Mussolini is told that his wish has been granted so promptly, he freely expresses his sense of satisfaction: "He's finally dead, that stiff-necked man!"

BUT THEN very quickly, within a month, the nuns are celebrating, their white habits fluttering about like doves, because of that wispy thread of smoke that colors the sky above Saint Peter's. *"Habemus papam, habemus papam,"* they exult, and Mother Cecilia, radiant with joy, clenches her hands into fists, her cheeks two apples shining with happiness. Even the mother superior comes down out of her tabernacle in the tower. The ancient lady walks down the gravel path of the garden to embrace first Mother Cecilia, then Mother Enrichetta and Mother Gregoria, her little fingers all wrinkled as they lie like insects on the white of their habits.

After only a one-day conclave, the Vatican secretary of state, Cardinal Eugenio Pacelli, son of a noble family from the province of Viterbo with close ties to the Curia, has been elected pope and taken the name of Pius XII. His cousin is Ernest Pacelli, who for many years has served as the managing director of the Banco di Roma, the bank that oversees the Vatican's finances. The new pope was nuncio to Germany from 1917 to 1929, first in Bavaria until 1920 and then in Berlin. And it was in Bavaria, in 1919, that he was present during a battle between the Bolsheviks and republican government troops. A group of Spartacist revolutionaries forcibly took refuge in the offices of the nunciature and, it seems, responded to his protests by pointing their guns at him.

It is an event that Pius XII will rarely mention but that remained so indelible as to make him deaf to the appeal of three Basque priests who came to the Vatican in 1937 after the bombing of Guernica, to deliver a letter from the vicar general of their dioceses to Pius XI. The three priests brought with them the testimony of nine fellow priests who were present at the massacre of the Basque people. When two of the three, Father Mancheca and Father Augustin Souci, arrived in Rome in April, Pacelli, then secretary of state, let them know through Monsignor Giuseppe Pizzardo that it was not necessary for them to be received by the pope since they had a letter. He would inform them as to how and when to deliver their appeal. For the next several days they heard nothing, until one morning as they were eating in a little neighborhood restaurant a messenger from the Vatican suddenly arrived in a great hurry, advising them that they were to be received by the secretary of state, on condition that the meeting remain secret and that they make no mention whatsoever of the reason they had come to Rome. Without even finishing their meal the priests followed him to the Vatican. The future Pius XII received them standing up. They mentioned the letter for the pope and immediately Pacelli, in a gelid voice,

showed them the door. "The Church is being persecuted in Barcelona," were the only words he said.

A ROBUST SISTER from Ebersberg who has been
in service with the new pope since 1917, when he was
nuncio in Bavaria, comes to the papal apartments to
oversee the preparation of food and keep the rooms in
order. She is a strong-willed, despotic woman, devout
to the point of fanaticism, whom the French cardinal
Eugène Tisserant will call "the popess." Who knows
what this Sister Pasqualina Lehnert (later Mother
Pasqualina) thinks of the banners outside Rosenheim, a
few kilometers from her hometown, with their slogans
against the contagion of the Jews.

The three nuns assigned to care for the personal needs
of the newly elected Pius XII must speak with him in German. Even more than my father, he admires the dedication
to work and the prodigious talent for order of the people
who live between the Rhine and the Vistula, the discipline
of their blond youth. He loves their language and their
customs, so much so that he decorates his Vatican apartment exclusively with mahogany furniture made in Germany, the work of German craftsmen. On one wall hangs
a large oil painting of the German school, and for dining
there are plates and glasses of German porcelain and crys-
tal, silverware made in Germany. The new pope also loves

birds, and two canaries who respond to the names Hansel and Gretel keep him company while he eats or works at his desk. Gretel, affectionately called Gretchen, is totally white and has a habit of perching on his papers.

In 1933 it was he, then secretary of state, who conducted the negotiations that led to the concordat between the Church and Hitler's Reich. (In 1947 he would justify it as an attempt "to save the concordats of the uncertain future, extending them geographically and substantively.") And the first diplomat to be received by the new pope is the German ambassador Diego von Bergen, while in a personal letter the Holy See himself informs Hitler of the positive outcome of the Vatican conclave. Mussolini, too, as soon as the white smoke wafts up into the sky over the dome of Saint Peter's, hurries to congratulate his colleague and comrade Hitler over the election of the former nuncio to Berlin.

The new secretary of state is Cardinal Luigi Maglione, who on orders from Pius XII instructs *L'Osservatore Romano* that from now on it is to avoid anti-German comments. At the same time attacks on the Vatican disappear from German newspapers.

And so it is amid almost unanimous jubilation that on March 12 steel trumpets announce the investiture of the new pope and the *coronam auream* descends slowly *super caput eius*. The celestial melodies of virgins and children rise through the immense nave of Saint Peter's Basilica as

the complete diplomatic corps lines its colors up alongside the purple of the College of Cardinals and an
impassioned crowd throngs Saint Peter's Square. Later
the streets of Rome swarm with festive flocks of priests
from the German College; they are young and dressed in
red with black belts around their waists—the same colors
as the flags of the Reich that hang limply from their
poles in this last season of peace.

IT WILL TAKE thirty-three years to know, at least in
part, what was on Pius XI's mind before he died and
what he probably intended to say to the bishops on February 11, 1939. And it will take fifty-six years before we
come to know the text of the encyclical *Humani generis
unitas* (The Unity of the Human Race), drafted at his
request by a French American Jesuit.

In 1938 John LaFarge, related on his mother's side to
Benjamin Franklin, is a young priest studying the question
of racism in the United States, particularly in Maryland,
where he lived until 1926. He has published a book called
Inter-racial Justice, which has established him as the fore-
most Catholic champion of the struggle for racial justice
in his country. On May 2, 1938, he lands in England on
the steamship *Volendam* to begin a report on the situation
in Europe for the Catholic weekly *America,* of which he is
the editor. He arrives in Rome on June 5, and just before

leaving again he is invited by the president of the Gregorian University, Father Vincent McCormack, to attend a general audience with the pope at Castel Gandolfo. A few days later, as he is getting ready to leave for Spain, a message arrives from the Vatican: the pope wishes to meet with him privately and has already arranged an appointment.

On the twenty-second LaFarge is back at Castel Gandolfo. Pius XI tells him that he has read *Inter-racial Justice* and thinks very highly of it. It's the best thing he's read on the subject, he declares. And just at the moment that he has been looking for a person to whom he can entrust the task that is closest to his heart, God has sent him Father LaFarge. Every day that goes by it seems to him that racism and nationalism are becoming more and more mixed up with each other, and the problem torments him constantly. Father LaFarge must prepare a draft for an encyclical on racism and promise to maintain absolute secrecy. The pope is aware that it would have been better to have first notified the father general of the Jesuits, but this way is all right too, he says. He will write to him that same day to inform him and ask him to provide Father LaFarge with all the necessary means to carry out the project. Then, having provided the general outlines of the argument, the method to follow, and the principles to observe, he adds, "simply say what you would say if you were pope."

For the young Jesuit it is "as if the Basilica of Saint Peter's had fallen on my head." On June 27, he meets with the father general of his order, the Polish Father Wladimir Ledochowski, who provides him with two collaborators, the German Jesuit Gustav Gundlach (the author of the anonymous radio broadcast on Vatican Radio several months earlier) and the French Jesuit Gustave Desbuquois, editor of the Paris-based review *L'Action Populaire*. They agree that once the draft has been completed LaFarge will bring it personally to Father Ledochowski, who will take responsibility for delivering it to Pius XI. Like the pope, the father general urges them to maintain secrecy. (He will insist on this again in the coming months, finding LaFarge to be insufficiently discreet.)

The three Jesuits start to work immediately in Paris. They are soon joined by another German Jesuit, Heinrich Bacht, whose task will be to translate the encyclical into Latin. In the heat of the summer, in less than three months, the English, French, and German drafts are completed. At least one of these versions bears the title *Humani generis unitas*. In September LaFarge leaves for Rome to deliver the draft to Father Ledochowski.

But the initial excitement of LaFarge and his collaborators gives way first to disappointment and finally to anxiety. Father Ledochowski seems to be in no particular hurry to deliver the document to Pius XI and says he has entrusted it to some experts. Actually, there is only one expert, Father Enrico Rosa, editor of *La Civiltà Cattolica,* who has been given an abridged version of the French draft. On October 1, two days after the Munich Pact between Hitler and Neville Chamberlain of Britain, and the same day that German troops occupy the Sudetenland, LaFarge embarks for the United States. On the sixteenth Gundlach, who has returned to Rome, writes to LaFarge urging him to communicate directly with Pius XI. His letter expresses his suspicion that Father Ledochowski is trying to "sabotage" their work "with a delaying action, for tactical and diplomatic reasons." In this letter, as in the ones that will follow, Pius XI and Father Ledochowski are never mentioned by name. The pope is M. Fisher (an allusion to his "fisher's" ring) and Ledochowski is sometimes Le Chef but more often L'Admodum.

But LaFarge hesitates to go over the head of his superior. On November 18 Gundlach writes to LaFarge again, informing him of his growing anxiety. The pope's health, he writes, is deteriorating rapidly and the surveillance around him is so strict "that by now nothing gets through to him except what they allow to get through to him." On the twenty-sixth Father Enrico Rosa dies after a long illness. The following February, when Pius XI dies, LaFarge, Gundlach, and Desbuquois are not even sure that the pope received their text. On March 2, with the election of Pius XII, the hopes of the three Jesuits are dashed. At the end of March 1939 Father Ledochowski informs them for the first time that their text was delivered to Pius XI just a few days before his death but that his successor has not yet had time to read it. In other words, the encyclical died before it was even born.

There are no witnesses and no evidence that Pius XI had the draft on his desk or, if he had it there, that someone saw it and set it aside after his death. It is as if the text had somehow sunk into unfathomable waters. The three Jesuits, bound by their promise to the pope, say nothing.

But in October 1939, when Pius XII promulgates his first encyclical, entitled *Summi pontificatus* (Of the Supreme Pontificate), some of the passages deploring the persecution of Polish Catholics will be taken entirely from the draft composed in Paris during the summer of 1938. Everything regarding the Jews and anti-Semitism, however, will have disappeared as will any mention of Nazism or of Hitler's policy of expansionism. For the moment there is not even a trace of much of *Humani generis unitas*.

And so it will remain until December 1972, when the American *National Catholic Reporter* will begin publishing extracts of a draft of an encyclical by Pius XI against racism. Of the original drafters only Father Heinrich Bacht will still be alive. Desbuquois will have died in 1959 and Gundlach and LaFarge in 1963. Putting LaFarge's papers in order in 1967, one of his former students, an American Jesuit named Thomas Breslin, will find fragments of the English draft of the encyclical and put them on microfilm. This is the document that will come into the possession of the *National Catholic Reporter*.

It will take another twenty years of stubborn and tireless research by two historians, Georges Passelecq, a Benedictine monk, and Bernard Suchecky, a Jewish historian of the social sciences and a librarian in Strasbourg, to discover at least one complete draft composed with such enthusiasm during the hot summer of 1938. Reconstructing the story is a long project that takes from 1987 to 1995, years spent running into continual refusals and postponements or sudden attacks of amnesia. Attempts to gain access to the Jesuit archives in Rome or to the Vatican archives are in vain; these have been closed to all inquiries since the death of Benedict XV in 1922.

Suchecky and Passelecq's book, *L'encyclique cachée de Pie XI,* reprints in an appendix the only full text that has been discovered up to now, the French draft, presumably the one given to Father Enrico Rosa, entitled *Humani generis unitas* (the German draft was entitled *Societatis unio*). There are about a hundred typed pages divided into 176 short chapters or paragraphs, the first 70 of which are edited and corrected in the recognizable style of Father Gundlach, the drafter who was most familiar with sociological and philosophical issues. The last part, rich in corrections, insertions, and annotations, more directly related to the situation of the Jews and to anti-Semitism, more pragmatic and specific, is probably the part that LaFarge dedicated himself to and that was subject to the most revision (perhaps Father Rosa, perhaps by LaFarge himself).

Today no one knows how much, and in what ways, *Humani generis unitas* could have changed the fate of millions of Jews. But certainly it would have constituted an inescapable problem of conscience for some 100 million European Catholics.

MEANWHILE, on March 15, 1939, German troops cross over the border of what is left of Czechoslovakia. This invasion of Bohemia and Moravia is carried out peacefully. But on September 1, when the German army enters Poland, it is war, although not for Italy, not for now. We are about to live our last nine months of peace.

Packed into the Astura, we are on our way from Ortisei to our house in Mirabello, near Monferrato in northwestern Italy. Along the way we stop to eat in Brescia, and in the sunny deserted piazza, in the shade of an orange umbrella, a voice booms out of a loudspeaker like a crashing black wave. Is it the voice of Hitler? I don't know. I only know that on that day and in that instant, the voice that means war cancels out every other sound. It is a voice that is dark, raspy, and sinister to my child's ears, as if I have become an adult the second those words start reverberating amid the empty tables. I am no longer the little girl with her spoon dipped in the warm soup; I am the look on the face of the waiter, standing there amazed with a plate in his hand, the sudden pallor of the owner sitting behind the cash register. Francesco, our driver, is alone at a table not far from ours, frozen with his fork in his hand and the spaghetti sliding off; Francesco, who suffered a broken leg in the First World War and who had to drag it behind him for four kilometers during the retreat at Caporetto.

Later, with my mother, I walk across the square. A few newspapers hang limply in front of the newsstand. With her I go into a fabric store and watch her select one roll of cloth after another—one with red and blue squares, one with flowers as thick as hedges, one with blue humming-birds. Yards and yards of cloth that she, a provident and wise mother, has the sales people unfurl on the counter, then cut with scissors that penetrate a little way, followed immediately by a long tear, a piercing, hissing sound. We leave the fabric store with the flies buzzing about on the wooden counter and go to buy shoes, which is harder. How do you know how much children's feet are going to grow? For me, the fun of a lazy summer afternoon has returned; the dark sinister voice, so shrill in the half-light of the restaraunt, has faded away. I enjoy trying on one pair of shoes after another, all scattered on the floor among the open boxes.

1 9 4 0 – 4 3

AT THE INSTITUTE on Corso d'Italia where I now go to school, the majority of the nuns are Italian but many of them have French names. The seasons follow each other in an unending ritual of prayers and "flowerets." That's what the nuns call the sacrifices that we are required to make. They dress in violet and on their fingers they each wear a thin circle of gold with a cross on it in witness to their matrimony with Christ, a little circle that taps metallically on the railing to call us to order on the stairway. Our uniforms are blue with gray kneesocks and black shoes. For chapel we have white organdy veils held at the back of our necks by an elastic band. When they're not on our heads the veils must be folded up inside a marbled cardboard case marked with a number. I'm given number 256. The number 256 is on my apron and on everything that apparently belongs to me—napkin ring, napkin, handkerchiefs—a number destined to follow me like a loyal dog for my remaining eleven years of school.

I go through the big iron gate at eight-twenty in the morning and I come out again at six in the evening. Sometimes it's still dark when we walk out the front door of our house and dark again when we come back in the evening. During the short break right after lunch we are allowed to let ourselves go what is supposed to be a playground but is really only a wedge of earth shaped like the prow of a ship stuck between Corso d'Italia and via Porta Pinciana. Besides the laurel and boxwood bushes there is just one tree. It's beautiful with a myriad of tiny little leaves, a pepper tree. The rest is dust enclosed by ten-foot-high walls. With our last bit of lunch still in our stomachs we have forty-five minutes to release all the energy that has been building up uncontrollably inside us hour after hour; then we go right back in with our uniforms smelling of sweat and our hands cold as ice. The day presses back down onto the gray classrooms whose windows are made of opaque glass to keep us from looking outside. But even more important they are to keep people on the outside from looking in at us. There is no sky and no leafy branches, just that dull hospital color.

Our desks, carved by the sharp pen points of genera-
tions of former students, are called *pupitres* and they have
covers that lift up to reveal notebooks and half-eaten
snacks nibbled on the sly. Every once in a while when
someone opens their desk cover the odor of overripe
orange peels wafts across the room. I hate that smell. And
I hate the morning smell of cabbage that heralds our
lunch at the long table in the refectory.

My teacher is Signorina Minchetti and starting in the
first month of school she gives me only an 8 for conduct
because I rock in my chair. In the afternoon, after I've
finished my homework, I shut myself in the bathroom
and stand on the toilet seat to look out the top part of the
window that has been cut away for ventilation. I can see
the grounds of the Villa Borghese and their winding dirt
paths, the light that looks almost azure as it slides down
the bark of the pine trees and softly onto the grass—the
azure blue of the sky that I can just barely glimpse. Some
children walk by hand in hand with adults, dogs run free
of their leashes. On a cement platform, day after day,
some workmen are building a cement pillbox.

A good floweret, says Mother Immaculée, might be
throwing candied fruit down the toilet, and her hand
with its pale butter skin makes the gesture of tossing it
into the toilet bowl. I don't like candied fruit but throwing it down the toilet is something I could never do.

Every so often Papa tells us about Rebuffi, the beggar who used to ring the doorbell to ask for a bowl of soup when Papa was a boy in Torino. *Rebuffi* has become a kind of code word; decoded it means, "You don't leave anything on your plate; food must be treated with respect because there are people dying of hunger who would be happy to eat what you waste by throwing it away." At the most, as a floweret for Lent, I can store up chocolate candy to eat at eleven o'clock on Easter Saturday, when the church bells ring to announce that Christ is risen.

In memory of his fasting in the desert we Christians, or the adults anyway, are obliged to fast during Lent, to eat just once a day and never meat or anything good. At my house, however, everyone has a "dispensation." Papa has stomach problems and if Mama doesn't eat she could faint. In the drawer of her night table there is always a little blue glass bottle of smelling salts to revive her. I don't know about Italia and Letizia. Italia says that for them it's always Lent anyway.

On Passion Sunday all the paintings in the church are covered with purple drapes, and the vestments of the priest who says Mass are also purple. During Lent it's not nice to play too much, tell jokes, laugh, or eat sweets. Each morning, as soon as we get to school, we go to chapel with our white veils on our heads to place at the foot of the cross our flowerets written on folded pieces of paper. During Lent we do spiritual exercises for three days with a priest named Father Pesce. There are no classes and no homework, and in the refectory we sit in silence and listen to the story of the life of Saint Tarcisio, the youth who was stoned for wanting to save the hosts with the body of Christ. Even when the fruit is served there is no *Deo gratias*. To me, *Deograzias* is a code word like *Rebuffi*. I still don't know Latin and to me it is a round sound that releases us from silence and instantly turns the refectory into an aviary. But during the spiritual exercises the only thing you can hear in the refectory is the sound of the silverware against the plates and the voice of Mother Rose reading. And the silence still follows us like an impalpable shadow in what is called the playground, where we are supposed not to play but to "meditate." I look at the pepper tree, its tiny light leaves, and I daydream. It doesn't grow fruit in the Roman climate, Mother Immaculée says. I imagine something shiny like the armored shell of a beetle.

In the chapel in the afternoon Father Pesce explains what Jesus expects of us: obedience, purity, and prayer. Our hearts are like a room that must be cleaned of all the dirt that has accumulated in the course of the year; it must become pure again like when we were baptized. And it's no use trying to be clever, he says, and just do a little dusting. Our mothers and Mother Immaculée might be fooled and not even notice if we tell them a lie.

But not God. He sees us all the time. "A black ant, on a black rock, in the darkest black night, and God sees him!" Father Pesce is skinny, and his round glasses reflect the light from the candles, pointing straight into our souls. I have an aching nostalgia for the plaster Christ who pointed to the naked heart on his chest, his chestnut hair flowing down to this shoulders. I don't like ants, and I prefer my guardian angel's big feathery wings to the eye of God. Father Pesce doesn't call them flowerets; he emphatically enunciates the word *sacrifices*. The son of God died because of us, he says, to save us. Look at him there hanging on the cross, and his finger points to the head resting on the chest lacerated by a long wound. The scribes and the Pharisees killed him, and we too with our sins. When we do bad things, when we tell even just one lie or when we have impure thoughts, then we are just like the scribes and the Pharisees, like Caiaphas and the crowd overflowing the square in Jerusalem yelling, "Death to the Nazarene! Death to the Nazarene!"

Then they whipped him with switches until he was bleeding and put a crown of thorns on his head, and the crowd mocked him, bringing down on themselves a terrible curse. Next they forced him to carry an immensely heavy cross on his shoulders way up to the top of Calvary, where he was to be put to death. And they nailed him to that cross, and when he grew thirsty and asked to drink they offered him, stuck on the end of a stick, a sponge steeped in vinegar, saying to him, "You are the son of God, save yourself!" And at the very moment that Christ died the sky grew dark, the curtain in the Temple of Jerusalem was rent in two, and Judas, who had betrayed him with a kiss, hung himself on a tree and went directly into the mouth of Lucifer. "Do we want to be like those scribes, those Pharisees, that crowd with the heart of stone yelling 'Death!'?" Behind his lenses Father Pesce's eyes are pinpoints that prick us between the ribs, searching to find the black ant on the black rock hidden in the dark night of our hearts. "Like Judas who gave his doleful name to the Judeans?" His voice ripples like a tremor. "Or do we want to be good Christians and make our hearts like tabernacles ready to welcome the son of God on the day of his Resurrection?"

Following behind him we have to walk to each of the fourteen stops of the Way of the Cross hanging on the walls. At each "station," representing one of the scenes of the cruel martyrdom of Christ, we kneel and recite one of the mysteries of the rosary. If anyone starts to look distracted, Mother Elena gives her a pinch, and if anyone talks, says even so much as a word, she yanks her out of the group and makes her kneel alone in the middle of the chapel.

Later on at home we have to sit in silence and think about the whipping and the crown of thorns, about the nails that pierced the hands and feet of Jesus. But a light signaling the coming of spring glances off the facade of the building across the street, the beans that I planted outside on the terrace have opened just a crack on two little round leaves, and the approaching darkness fills via Flaminia with voices and the sound of front doors slamming shut. In the picture with the blue frame the little girl with the red beret skates on a frozen lake surrounded by mountains. In the kitchen Letizia flips the jelly-filled pancakes; *omelettes confiture,* Mama calls them. And so it is hard to keep thinking about the nails and the cross and the crown of thorns. Mama does spiritual exercises too, at the church of San Carlo on the Corso, but then when she comes home she talks on the phone and tells Letizia to fill the pancakes with strawberry jelly.

I would like to know if Judeans and Jews are the same thing. Mama says yes, they're the same, but we should always say Jews because Judeans isn't a nice word, and it's vulgar. Someone might be offended.

On Holy Thursday I go with her and Papa to visit the sepulchers, three or five but almost always seven because it has to be an odd number. It's not hard to find seven churches in the area between piazza del Popolo and the Corso, and the streets are filled with people going in and out of church doors amid the glow from the wax candles lit up around the sepulchers. Some of the people we run into are friends of Mama and Papa's and they stop to say hello. I look at their children and their children look at me. The sepulcher I always like best is the one in Santa Maria del Popolo that has a carpet in front of it made of a special grass, almost white, that grows in the dark. The warm light of the candle flames shines all around it, and as we come out of the church we start to breathe the holiday air, a smell that reminds me of the sea. In each church I get to light a candle and it would be lovely if Holy Thursday afternoon never ended, if it didn't lead right into that Friday of gloom when we have to stand immobile in the chapel for the entire reading of the Passion of Our Lord Jesus while Mother Elena stares at us with her coal-black eyes. There is almost always rain and the sky is a lurid gray, and three in the afternoon, when Jesus exhales his last breath, seems never to arrive. But later the day is really beautiful; Jesus has finished suffering and, wrapped in the burial shroud, he goes to rest in the sepulcher of Joseph of Arimathea and the nuns send us home.

We walk down through the Villa Borghese. The moss is like velvet on the stone of the Fiocco Fountain and the tall oak trees cover the ground with a purple shade. Our current fräulein is a fervent and naïve Czechoslovakian virgin with braids wrapped around her head, and as we walk she urges us to breathe deeply to free our lungs of all the bad air they've accumulated during the course of the day. I try to imitate her, staring at her chest that swells up to an enormous size under her tight blue overcoat, the features of her Slavic face flushed with color and revived by the effort of her breathing.

The Jews have Easter too, Mother Immaculée says, but it has nothing to do with our holy day. They don't believe that Christ rose from the dead or that he was the son of God. Then what about all those signs—the darkened sky, the curtain in the temple torn in two? Mother Immaculée's face is like a big egg, her nose is shiny, and she smiles a lot, showing the compact round curve of her teeth. But now her lips are stretched tight and she looks like she's ready to suck in all the air around her. "There is none so blind as those who will not see," she says, "or deaf as those who will not hear." Well, then, what kind of Easter do they celebrate? Certainly not the Resurrection, since they're the ones who killed Christ! Mother Immaculée doesn't say that, I do. And I'm proud of my cleverness. The Jews' Easter isn't a real Easter. There are no church bells, no lamb, no chocolate eggs. They don't even have those little sheep made of sugar with a red ribbon tied around their necks.

I DON'T KNOW what these first days of war are like for the Levi boy. Next door, where Signora Della Seta lives with her brother, silence has filled the apartment like a wad of cotton. The winter of 1939–40 has made a sinister entrance into their lives. The Race Tribunal has been functioning for several months now, and the Della Setas can't leave their homes without the advance permission of the public safety authorities. They no longer have passports; what would they use them for anyway? The news from Germany is increasingly bleak.

I have a new friend who has the same name as the street I live on: Flaminia. Her governess is French and she calls her Mademoiselle. When we go skating at the Circus Maximus, Mademoiselle wears a mouse-colored felt hat and doesn't speak to anyone as she follows Flaminia step by step along the edge of the skating rink. Flaminia has black ringlets and a beaver bolero; at the wedding of the king's youngest daughter she was one of the bridesmaids. In her house a photo shows her beside the royal bride with a long dress down to her feet and a crown of roses atop her black curls, her arms left bare by the short, puffy sleeves. In other photographs displayed here and there on the furniture the princess of Piemonte has eyes as clear as stones from a riverbed while the prince looks across at her from the piano, tall and handsome in his uniform; the dedication is decorously royal. The Duce is present as well, seated at his work table at the Palazzo Venezia, the unmistakable *M* of the hurried signature typical of an anointed world leader. Flaminia also has a dog, a fox terrier, and she combs him with a silver comb that she keeps in the bathroom. As our playroom we're permitted to use a walk-in closet protected by red curtains, where there are evening dresses and old velvet capes, big hats with feathers in them. For our snack Zeno, the cook, makes us a loaf of bread served in thin slices, and between each slice we have prosciutto or salami, or mayonnaise and pickles. Even Olga, the maid, must be really rich since as a First Communion present she gave Flaminia a rooster pin with a body made of a big natural pearl. We play dress-up assisted by Mademoiselle and Flaminia always insists on giving herself the part of the fairy or the queen.

Flaminia is the youngest daughter of the new friends my parents met in Cortina during Christmas vacation. Mama and Papa liked their new friends and Cortina so much that this summer we're all going together to stay in two houses not far from each other along the road that goes from Cortina up to Pomagnon. For now they have taken two neighboring boxes at the opera and every Sunday we meet at the theater. Mama has had her seamstress make us bordeaux velvet dresses with lace collars and caps made of the same material for our heads. Flaminia, on the other hand, has a lot of light satin dresses, yellow, pastel green, or light blue, with short knee-length skirts, over which she wears hand-knitted angora sweaters. Sitting still in the box is unbearable for me and time refuses to pass. Unfortunately I don't understand anything about music and what affects me most is the horrible sight of those big-bellied tenors and the sopranos shaking with fat. With my eyes fixed on the clock above the stage, I wait for the instant, every five minutes, when the hands jump forward. Until intermission. Then Flaminia and I are let loose to run up and down the corridors, peeking into the boxes at people we don't know. We open the doors and slam them shut and run away before the disapproving glances in our direction can take the form of a reprimand. Our parents all move into one box to chat and Flaminia's mother offers around some new candies wrapped in silver paper with "You and Me" written on it. I don't like them because they taste like licorice but I pretend they are wonderful.

Flaminia's parents know a lot of important people and they are sure that the Germans will win the war quickly because they are so orderly and so well-disciplined and the English don't really want to fight, all they know how to do is command. This Flaminia's parents know because their eldest son is engaged to an English girl (her picture is in the living room, too, with her head tilted to one side). But now that the English are about to become our enemies the engagement may have to be called off. They think very highly of Mussolini and they use the newly fashionable *"voi"* form of address with the usher who opens the boxes. But Papa says it's better not to talk about politics. Mama and her new friend use the familiar *"tu"* form. Papa still uses the formal *"lei"* with everyone because, he says, that's what he's used to. He only uses *"tu"* sometimes with some of his workers, when he can see that they feel more comfortable that way.

ON MAY 12, 1940, after raining down a tempest of bombs during the night on the Dutch city of Rotterdam, Germany invades Belgium, Holland, and Luxembourg. The next day *L'Osservatore Romano* publishes the texts of three telegrams sent by Pius XII to the three helpless victims of aggression. Several newsstands that sell the Catholic daily are vandalized by thugs on orders from Roberto Farinacci, publisher of *Il Regime Fascista.* The attacks are a clear sign that our Duce has decided that he's not going to remain an idle spectator of Hitler's land grab for much longer but will try to take a seat at the banquet table before it's too late.

Schools close ahead of schedule and by the first week of June we are already in Ostia, by the sea. On the eighth, the apostolic nuncio in Berlin, Monsignor Cesare Orsenigo, informs Ernst Wormann, a representative of the German Foreign Ministry, of his desire that Italy enter the war and congratulates Germany on its victories. Joking, he then adds his wish that the Germans will enter Paris from Versailles.

On the afternoon of June 10, from the balcony of the Palazzo Venezia, greeted by thunderous applause, Mussolini announces to the citizens of the peninsula that they are now at war with France and England. My brother, who had gone out to buy himself a soccer ball is picked up and forced to join a demonstration headed by the local butcher in Ostia. He's taken to the front of a house inhabited by an Englishman to yell insults under his window. It's a really hot day and with the excuse that he wants to get a drink from a nearby fountain he manages to get away. The ball, white and blue like the colors of the Lazio football team, is saved too. That evening Papa goes to visit Signora Fioravanti, who is French, to express his solidarity and his shame as an Italian citizen for what, for decades to come, will be known as "the knife in the back."

The next day Cardinal Tisserant of France sends a dramatic letter to his countryman Cardinal Emmanuel Suhard about the Fascist and Hitlerian ideology that has transformed the consciences of young people. "Those under thirty-five years old," he writes, "will go along with anything. . . . I have persistently asked the Holy See since the beginning of December to publish an encyclical on the duty of each individual to obey the dictates of conscience, because it is a vital point of the Christian faith. . . . I fear that history will reproach the Holy See for having pursued policies of selfish convenience and not much more. It is very sad for those of us who lived under Pius XI."

At dawn on June 14 German advance troops under Georg von Küchler enter Paris and soldiers on horseback parade through the Arc de Triomphe. A few days later Hitler makes a blitz visit to the French capital. At six in the morning his black Mercedes convertible drives along the still-deserted streets and boulevards up to the top of Montmartre. From the heights of the white church of Sacré Coeur, with the Eiffel Tower barely visible in the early light, the chancellor of the Reich surveys his newly conquered domain. Before the sun is high in the sky Hitler has already gone, and Paris will never see him again.

France has been divided into two zones, the bigger one, in the north, occupied by the troops of the Reich. The second, the southwest, with Vichy as its capital, remains under French jurisdiction. The government of the so-called free zone, under President Philippe Pétain (a hero of the First World War) and Prime Minister Pierre Laval (a former Socialist member of Parliament now in the ranks of the far right), doesn't lose any time. On October 3 it approves anti-Semitic legislation modeled after the Fascist racial laws. Especially restrictive measures are adopted against the numerous Jews who between 1933 and 1939 had sought refuge in France, trusting in the security of the Maginot Line and in the country's hallowed liberal tradition.

The new French ambassador to the Vatican, Léon
Bérard, requests an official statement of the Vatican's position on the measures adopted by his government. The
answer is a reassuring message for Laval and Pétain: "In a
Christian state it would make no sense to allow the levers
of power to rest in the hands of the Jews, thus limiting the
authority of Catholics. It is therefore legitimate to deny
them access to public office and to give them a limited
number of places in the universities and the professions."

THE WAR still doesn't concern me and I sometimes
even find it thrilling. The first night that the alarm
sounds for a French airplane dropping leaflets over
Rome I start jumping up and down on the bed with
excitement. And when we arrive in Cortina at the end
of July I am enchanted looking out over the valley that
the absence of lights has turned into a kind of manger
scene, with the moon popping up over the mountains.

We children are rehearsing a play to celebrate Flaminia's mother's patron saint's day. We've decided to put
on *Principe Ranocchio* (The Frog Prince) and naturally
Flaminia has the part of the princess. I'm a servant
whose only line is, "There's a man with a little box."

Flaminia's parents are still sure that the war will last no
more than a couple of seasons. As we wait for news of

our soldiers' successes, we declare war on the children of a neighboring house and we exchange insulting messages with them that we stick on the trees. I manage to get my nose broken in most inglorious fashion. My brother, ordering me to go and get a message that's been stuck to a tree trunk, turns toward me with such uncontrolled force that the stick in his hand hits me right on the bridge of the nose.

But love also has its part in this first summer of war, and when my oldest sister and a bunch of her friends declare themselves enamored of a boy by the name of Rienzi, I try to include myself in the group by saying that I, too, am in love with him. And even though I'm the youngest I still succeed in getting a kiss, although to get it I have to climb up on a stool. The emotion felt is zero, but the exhibition is very gratifying.

It is a beautiful summer. As predicted, Flaminia's big brother has broken off his engagement with the English girl and has enrolled in an officers' training course. The other brother, reputedly a real ladies' man, is courting a nineteen-year-old who is considered quite brazen because she wears flannel trousers and paints her fingernails red. Flaminia and I spy on them but we don't manage to see anything more than their occasionally holding hands.

The most spectacular news comes at the end of August: Flaminia's mother is expecting a baby. Neither Flaminia nor I know yet what the cause is of such an effect, nor do we know the exact location of the future child. We must have some notion in our heads, however, because with the bathroom door closed, Flaminia takes off her underpants and lets me see her little round behind. When it's my turn I pull mine down just far enough to uncover my groin, refusing to show anything else. I believe in fact that my behind parts are much more private and important.

With Italy's entry into war, Jews defined as "foreigners" (refugees from Nazi-occupied countries but also those who acquired Italian citizenship after 1919) are arrested and handcuffed and taken to internment camps. The order also includes Jews from allied countries, such as Germans and Czechoslovakians. In the meantime, an interminable series of circulars has begun to make life more and more difficult for Italian Jews. While the early measures were meant to isolate them, the steadily increasing number of prohibitions imposed by the Ministry of Internal Affairs are aimed at making it harder and harder for them to work and thus at making their survival more and more precarious. Every time a "person of Jewish race" asks for a license to engage in some activity, a circular issued ad hoc prohibits it. Jews are prohibited, month by month, from dealing in precious stones, taking photographs or doing anything else with cameras, acting as agents or brokers. From engaging in typographic work, selling art or antiques, selling books, used goods, children's toys, playing cards, or stationery. Selling eyeglasses or other optical devices, managing deposits or engaging in the resale of calcium carbide, running wine shops or liquor stores. They are prohibited from picking up scrap metal or metal of any other kind, wool for mattresses, trash or garbage. From collecting and reselling articles of military surplus. They are prohibited from operating dancing schools, sewing classes, travel agencies, or tourist bureaus. From renting films. From obtaining amateur fishing licenses or licenses to operate taxis. From giving private lessons to non-Jewish students. From entering the stock exchange or public libraries. From being members of cooperatives, cultural associations, or sporting clubs. From being members of the Society for the Prevention of Cruelty to Animals. From working as guides or interpreters. From raising carrier pigeons.

THE HAPPY EVENT in Flaminia's house takes place at the end of the year. The baby is a girl and the name Maria Vittoria is bestowed on her in honor, and as a portent, of the victory that appears imminent. The Duce sends a telegram with his best wishes.

Since October 15, the EIAR, the Italian broadcasting authority, has been airing a new series of ten-minute broadcasts each Wednesday at 7:30 p.m. under the direction of the Ministry of Popular Culture. The show is called *The Protocols of the Elders of Zion.*

The New Year's Eve that ushers out 1940 and welcomes 1941 finds Italians still optimistic and ready to celebrate with wine, domestic *spumante,* or French champagne, depending on their means. The pope has a cordial visit with the Reich's ambassador to the Vatican, Diego von Bergen, during which he expresses his congratulations for Germany's victories in a long speech delivered in German.

On March 21, the first day of spring, the Lisbon newspaper *A Voz* reports that seven hundred priests have been killed in the concentration camps of Oranienburg, Dachau, Buchenwald, and Auschwitz, and another three thousand are still detained. The news of the torture, deportation, and murder of Polish clerics who refuse to subject themselves to the ruthless demands of the invaders are by now no secret to the Vatican.

But no official protest is sent to Berlin, while insistent rumors continue to circulate of an imminent German attack to the east, in the direction of the Soviet Union.

Operation Barbarossa begins on June 22. Three armies, 110 divisions in all, attack the Soviet Union across a wide front, and in just a few days they take the part of Poland under Soviet control and move into the Ukraine. Some 260,000 Italian soldiers depart in support of their German comrades in arms, who are once again victorious. And peace, which only a few months ago seemed just around the corner, begins slowly to move into the distance, pulled by the troop trains that, in the heat and dust of summer, transport our soldiers—World War I rifles on their shoulders, their legs wrapped in cloth—thousands of kilometers from home, to a country that they find hard even to recognize on the map.

The Vatican does not hide its satisfaction over the attack on the Soviet Union and the brilliant German victories. And although up until June 22, in more or less veiled terms, Vatican Radio had continued to mention the suffering of the Polish Church, after the start of the Russian campaign all unfavorable allusions to the Reich disappear from its broadcasts. On June 26 Ambassador von Bergen is able to write to Berlin: "The nuncio asked me today if we still had complaints to make about Vatican Radio. I told him that we did not." And notwithstanding the large number of priests imprisoned and deported by the Germans (at Dachau alone, the Americans would find 326 priests still in the camp in 1945), no voices are raised to denounce the concordat that Monsignor Pacelli signed just eight years earlier and that Hitler betrays whenever and however he wants.

In an address on June 29, broadcast on the radio in honor of the feast of Saints Peter and Paul, Pius XII declares: "Still, in the darkness of the storm, there are some breaks in the clouds that lift our spirits toward great and holy hopes, a generous courage in the service of the defense of the fundamental values of Christian culture and a sure hope in its triumph." The pope's words seem to Ambassador von Bergen to augur well, and he reports them in his dispatch to Berlin. "Pius XII wished to express," he writes, "the hope that the great sacrifices required by the war will not be useless and will lead to victory over bolshevism, in accordance with the will of Providence."

The forty million Catholics living in the vast territory controlled by the Reich, which by now has extended its power over France, Belgium, Holland, Luxembourg, and Poland as well as Denmark and Norway, can sleep soundly and celebrate the extraordinary victories of the German armies advancing eastward, apparently unstoppable.

AT THE END of the school year we are taken to the Vatican to be received in a private audience by the pope. It is a rare privilege that Pius XII concedes to our institution, where he served as spiritual counselor when he was a young priest at the beginning of his career. Back then, he used to come once a week to hear the confessions of the nuns consecrated to Holy Mary Assumed into Heaven. For the sisters who knew him then to see him again as pope is an indescribable emotion, and, starting at eight o'clock in the morning, we are lined up in double file to practice again and again our curtsies, songs, and genuflections, dressed in our cream-white uniforms that we wear for special occasions. And we sweat and sweat. The nuns sweat too: pearl-like drops run down Mother Immaculée's long, damp nose and Mother Elena's straight, pointed one that is always shaking. Even Mother Superior's intrusive nose, like an anteater's, is covered with little droplets as she moves around us like a periscope, seeking to discern the slightest mark on the white of our socks or a ribbon tied too loosely around our braids.

The June sun beats down on the stones of Saint Peter's Square, where the pointed shadow of the obelisk looks like the needle of a sundial as we pass double file in front of the Swiss Guards with their halberds red-hot from the heat. The "daughters of Mary" are in the lead with their tin medals hung from large light blue ribbons bouncing on their chests (the supreme honor). Next come the "aspirants," who more modestly let swing from a small purple and white ribbon a medal of much smaller dimensions. In this semimilitary hierarchy, I hide myself among the troops without rank, unworthy even of the little pin carrying a merit badge.

The memory I keep of Pius XII is circumfused by a sacred halo. Everything is white and blurry, as if we were immersed in whiteness just like the bad children that big

Nikolas dipped in the ink. We are good and full of flowerets. I'm supposed to ask for "grace," but I don't remember now which kind. The words get stuck on my lips and I resort to the simplest pat phrase: "I don't want to tell lies anymore," I stammer. The floors sparkle with light, the sun is brutal, all around us the painted walls are as luminous as the skies of paradise. The pope slips a gold-embossed white envelope into my hands. Later, a rosary that looks like mother-of-pearl but may be made of Galalith, slides out of the envelope; its value is beyond estimation.

In the photograph taken in the square in front of the basilica the pope isn't there. I'm on one side, in the second row with my white veil stiff with starch. The nuns aren't in the picture either. In the photograph there is no more trace of the halo, no sign of the sacred, just a white pyramid of little girls that ends at the top with the bigger girls, standing full-breasted against the pale gray of the facade. On the side stands Signorina Garroni, a teacher, in black with a black lace veil on her head.

IN AUGUST Father Maximilian Kolbe, a Polish priest, dies at Auschwitz. He dies more or less upright although one can't really say on his feet, because the bones in his legs have been broken. The camp's "hunger bunker" is in fact a kind of vertical coffin that doesn't allow any other positions. He dies because one of the prisoners has escaped and the reprisal devised by the SS officer in charge of the camp calls for ten prisoners from the escapee's cell block to be beaten with clubs until their bones are broken, then walled up inside these narrow vertical cells to die of hunger and thirst. Father Kolbe volunteered to take the place of one of the selected prisoners.

In September, in Germany and throughout the territories under the jurisdiction of the Reich, all Jews over the age of six are ordered to wear a clearly visible star made of yellow cloth, sewn onto their clothes so they can be identified at all times. The next year, in June 1942, the same measure will be extended to all occupied territories.

Also in September 1941, the blitzkrieg begins to lose its momentum, first in the mud and then in the snow. Trapped in the deep freeze of the terrible Russian winter, in temperatures of fifty below zero, Hitler's armies come to a halt a few kilometers outside of Moscow, just short of the distant profile of its onion domes, visible in the crystal-clear wind-blown days of winter. The troops will start to move again, pursued by the Soviet army, at the beginning of December, to retreat, ruinously and dramatically, in the winter of 1942–43. In five years of war the number of European dead will come to more than fifty million; the exact figure will be impossible to determine.

But in November 1941 Pius XII can still express to the Spanish ambassador to the Vatican, Yangus Messia, his warmest sympathy for Germany and his admiration for the Führer's outstanding qualities. Conveyed to Ambassador von Bergen, the pope's sentiments are relayed to Berlin by him in a satisfied telegram on the seventeenth.

On November 29 Pietro Fedele, secretary of Herald's College, requests an audience with Pius XII. He has been charged by the king to inform the pope that His Majesty intends to confer the title of prince on the Pacelli family, in the person of His Holiness's nephews, the sons of his brother Francesco. This is an unusual gesture and the reasons for this special benevolence on the part of Victor Emmanuel III, well known to be a Mason, are unclear. Pius XII is grateful for the honor and naturally accepts.

In Berlin, in the meantime, on the eleventh of that month, a sixty-six-year-old priest, Bernhard Lichtenberg, prior of the chapter of canons of Saint Hedwig's Cathedral in Berlin (author of the only public protest against the events of *Kristallnacht*), offers a prayer for the Jews, both baptized and unbaptized, at the evening service. The police search his apartment and find the draft of another sermon, this one warning the faithful not to believe the regime's accusations against the Jews. They arrest him. The papal nuncio in Berlin, Monsignor Orsenigo, does not even request to be informed of the reasons the prior of the cathedral has been put in jail. Lichtenberg asks to be sent to the East with the Jews so as to pray with them in some faraway place. Sentenced to two years in jail, he will be released on October 23, 1943, and handed over to the Gestapo to be sent to Dachau. He will die before arriving at his destination.

THE TURNING POINT comes on December 7, 1941. The Japanese launch a surprise attack, bombing and in large part destroying the American fleet anchored in Pearl Harbor. The United States, which until that moment had limited itself to offering substantial material and moral support to England and the Soviet Union, finds itself at the center of conflict. Germany and Italy immediately side with their Japanese ally and, in turn, declare war on the United States.

But although Churchill's response to the news of the attack on Pearl Harbor is to throw his hat into the air with a symbolic hurrah, the United States's entry into the war does not provoke the same enthusiasm in the Vatican. Now there is fear of a German rout with the consequent reinforcement of the "gigantic Soviet octopus"—an octopus that, with its bloody tentacles, continues to look threateningly at us from propaganda posters plastered on the city's walls.

Still, nothing disturbs the order in via Flaminia. Giorgio Levi's mother, who before she was married was graduated from Cambridge, has begun giving English lessons. She is only permitted to have Jewish students, and Elsa, the concierge, stands watch over the racial morality of our building. Giorgio attends a school set up by the Jewish community in the Trastevere neighborhood and he leaves for school very early each morning on his bicycle with a scarf around his neck. Sometimes as I ride, still sleepy-eyed, on our school bus I can see him peddling quickly along the river road, his bicycle bouncing over the tram tracks. Our school bus winds along a long route before stopping at the black gate in Corso d'Italia and it fills up well beyond its limit, with the smallest children forced to ride in the arms of the bigger ones, who torment them with pinches. Fortunately I'm ten years old now and no longer subject to the pinching. I'm in the fourth grade and my teacher is Signorina Garroni, a sort of lay nun, old and fat, who keeps her false teeth in place by chewing on blotting paper that she hides in her desk drawer. My monthly report card almost always bears the comment "Can do more." It's my little bugaboo that comes and goes like the 8 for conduct that Papa finds completely unsatisfactory. Because of the new food rationing system, and to my boundless joy, we no longer eat cabbage and rice together with the boarding students. Instead we carry our lunch from home and eat in a separate room with a few other members of the elect. Letizia makes us spinach omelets and baked potatoes, and when we open the metal lunch box the consoling smell of homemade food wafts into the air.

During religion class a beautiful little girl with light brown skin and a thin nose sits next to me. She doesn't wear a uniform and she has a strange name that sounds like it comes from the delta of the Nile. I'm fascinated by her silence. She has thin, pointy, restless hands that write listlessly in a notebook. When we leave the room a governess comes for her dressed in a severe blue dress and matching veil, and together they get into a closed carriage, a landau, with a noble family crest painted on the door. One afternoon I get a glimpse of a woman inside with the same thin, smooth-skinned face surrounded by a collar of gray fox. Then all of a sudden one afternoon, taking advantage of Mother Immaculée's momentary absence, my bench mate starts talking and she tells me that she comes to religion class because she has to make her First Communion. But she's never been to school and she may never go at all. She studies at home and is an only child, and her slightly raised upper lip reveals small white pointed teeth. But as soon as Mother Immaculée comes back in the room she turns mute again, her mouth contracted just a little bit in a complicit smile that does not involve her eyes, which have gone back to staring straight ahead without expression. And that lip now raised just a little too high over her teeth makes her smile a little cruel, but unhappy as well.

Then, before Christmas, from one day to the next, just as she had come, she disappears. The vacant *pupitre* turns into a hole through which she has disappeared to be lost in the entrails of the earth, where she is racing now in her landau with her puffy-chested driver in the coach box. Inside her desk she has left a wooden case with a pencil and an eraser that I don't dare touch.

When I come back to school after Christmas vacation my bench mate is once again Maria Luisa Rosi, who talks incessantly, holding her hand in front of her mouth so she won't be seen. And when Mother Immaculée turns her back to the class, she lifts up the cover of her *pupitre* and bites voraciously into her snack with a shower of bread crumbs.

Although my aristocratic and ephemeral former bench mate is undoubtedly Aryan, she is only the first of a series of fleeting apparitions that will multiply the following year and reach their peak during the winter of 1943–44, when students with invented names will enliven the cold gray atmosphere of the school day, new classmates with Tuscan or Triestan accents whose backgrounds will be all the more interesting because they are both varied and vague at the same time. They will be the daughters of mixed marriages or even of two Jews, some hurriedly baptized and all of them outfitted with emergency uniforms.

ON JANUARY 20, 1942, at a conference held at Wannsee, as the Reich's highest-ranking political officials look out over the beautiful lakes and forests surrounding Berlin, a secret decision is made with regard to the Jews, the Final Solution, a pale euphemism for their complete extermination.

Not that mass slaughters have not already been carried out. Since the spring of 1941, when *Einsatzgruppen* were established, some 800,000 people have been killed, primarily Communists and Jews, from the countries of Eastern Europe. But the Final Solution calls for the death of eleven million Jews, and the organization set up to carry out the operation must be perfect and extremely efficient and fast. To overcome the obstacle represented by the physical elimination of millions of people it is decided to construct a model extermination camp at Birkenau, a few kilometers from Auschwitz, where the I. G. Farben chemical company has posted over the entrance in wrought-iron letters the slogan *Arbeit Macht Frei,* the same slogan that hangs over each of its factories. On this desolate, windblown plain in Poland now annexed to the Reich, where Oswiecim has been rebaptized Auschwitz, the tracks for the trains carrying deportees will stop, by

April 1944, in front of the five crematoria of Birkenau (or Auschwitz II). Specially built elevators will connect the ovens to a lower level of gas chambers disguised as showers, where openings in the showerheads will emit Zyklon B, a gas that takes at most fifteen minutes to kill. The trauma for the executioners will be reduced to the bare minimum. A previous system of executions, conducted in trucks with the direct emission of gas into air-tight containers built to order by the Diamond, Opel-Blitz, and Sauer companies, produces an insufficient number of deaths, even when operating at full capacity. Furthermore, when used in the autumn of 1941 in Chelmno, near Lodz, the trucks prove to be impractical because death came very slowly and the subsequent unloading of the corpses presented a number of problems.

Additional extermination camps are erected at Belsec (it will become "operative" in March 1942), Sobibor (operative in May), and Treblinka (operative in July).

The Final Solution is broken down into four stages. First the victims are registered, then they are stripped of their property, then they are deprived of their freedom of movement, and lastly they are deported to be exterminated. The cost of their rail transport will have to be financed by the Jews themselves, by confiscating any possessions they still have at the moment of deportation. The German railroads, which offer a group fare for a minimum of four hundred deportees, will receive the proceeds from the sale of wedding rings and gold teeth removed from the victims before they are put into the cremation ovens.

IT HAS never been clearly established when and how the news of the systematic extermination of the Jews became known in the Vatican. On February 9, 1942, in any event, Monsignor Orsenigo, papal nuncio in Berlin, requests that priests detained in the camp at Auschwitz be transferred to Dachau.

On February 29, the archbishop of Crakow, Adam Sapieha, writes a letter to the pope in Latin denouncing the horrible crimes inflicted on the citizens and clerics of Poland. The tragic tone of his letter reflects the fact that there is not enough food for survival. The archbishop entrusts the letter to Father Pirro Scavizzi, military chaplain of a hospital train operated by the Order of Malta, so he can take it to Rome.

But the next day the archbishop changes his mind and sends a Dominican priest, Father Voroniewsky, to ask Father Scavizzi to destroy the letter. He is afraid of Nazi reprisals and feels that not only he but the entire Polish clergy are too vulnerable. Father Scavizzi obeys and burns the letter, but first he copies it and leaves for Rome with the copy in his pocket. Pius XII will read the letter a few days later and Father Scavizzi will describe for him what is happening in Poland. "There are some who would ask for nothing less than the excommunication of Hitler and his followers," Father Scavizzi will recall himself saying. "Moved and agitated" by the dramatic account, Pius XII will raise his hands to the sky. "Tell everyone," he will respond, "everyone you can, that the pope is in agony for them and with them!"

On the official level, however, there is no record of any protest, much less of any spoken or written pronouncement. No such condemnation will be issued for the entire duration of the war, even though in Poland, in the part annexed to the Reich as Warthegau, five out of six bishops are interned or deported and most of the almost two thousand priests are no longer able to perform their duties because they have been arrested or locked up in concentration camps. (Pius XII will excommunicate all Communists in 1949 and that same year will excommunicate those responsible for the arrest of Cardinal József Mindszenty in Hungary. In 1955 it will be the turn of Argentine leader Juan Perón.) Not even loyal Mother Pasqualina speaks in her memoirs about the letter delivered by Father Scavizzi, but on the death of Pius XII she will burn two entire sacks of documents. On November 8, 1942, Archbishop Sapieha will write in protest to Hans Frank, governor-general of Poland: "I will not go into the atrociousness of using the young drunks of the national labor service in the extermination of the Jews."

It remains rather curious, however, that for the entire year 1942 the Catholic Church of Germany will continue to receive from Hitler's Reich some 900 million marks as a contribution to the faith.

IN MAY 1942, Italy adopts a program of civil conscription for Jews. The decision, according to the Ministry of Demography and Race, is meant to redress the preferential treatment accorded to Jews, "who, free from the obligation of military service, are able to dedicate themselves to financial speculation and idleness, to leading the good life, which necessarily offends the fighting and working masses of Italians, who are giving their all to the cause of victory." The measure involves all Jews of both sexes, from eighteen to fifty-five years of age, including those exempt from other sanctions. In the assignment of jobs, preference is given to manual labor and, in any case, the jobs must not be among those already prohibited for Jews. Compensation is limited to almost half the ordinary wage and will be gradually reduced to a quarter. The Ministry of Internal Affairs recommends jobs such as digging and clearing drainage ditches, street cleaning, apple harvesting, and packing up fruit at produce markets. Also the removal of rubble and debris—since we have been at war with the United States our cities have become a constant target for the American air force. This type of conscription will meet with very little enthusiasm from local prefects, however, because of the difficulties of employing a workforce that is so heterogeneous with respect to age and ability.

On July 16–17 the Nazis shift their attention from east to west: the first deportations of "stateless" Jews (those who have emigrated since 1919) are ordered in occupied Holland and France. But on August 26, in a surprise move that will remain unique in all of Europe, police in the free French zone arrest Jews in areas under their control. The Jews are loaded onto trains and shipped over the line of demarcation, to be handed over to the German authorities, who will deport them to Auschwitz.

The voice of protest from the French clergy makes itself heard immediately. The archbishop of Toulouse, Jules-Gérard Saliège, sends a letter to the parish priests of his diocese urging them to express their dissent from the pulpit. The same action is taken by the archbishop of Lyon and the bishop of Montauban. In Lyon a number of priests are arrested for reading the archbishop's letter to the faithful and for sheltering Jews in church buildings. As early as June 14, Father Dilland of the church of

Saint Louis in Vichy, who will die in Dachau for hiding eighty Jewish children, has invited the faithful to pray for the thousands of scorned French citizens obliged to wear the yellow star. Risking their lives, the parish priests of Saint Lambert and Saint Etienne du Mont protest in Paris. The pastor of Saint Pierre du Gros Caillou is to the point: "My sermon will be short. I know that it will cost me detention in a concentration camp. But it is my duty to repeat this: Pius XI condemned racism. Amen."

But not everyone agrees. As the letter of the archbishop of Toulouse reaches its destinations, the bishops of Nice, Monaco, and Fréjus and the abbots of Leyrins and Fregolet send a telegram to Marshal Pétain dissociating themselves from those Catholics, poor patriots, whose apparent preoccupation with the Jews is just a mask for their lack of faith in the regime.

The Vatican is silent. On July 30 Harold Tittmann, the acting American representative to the Holy See, sends a telegram to the State Department in Washington reporting that he has tried on several occasions to bring to the attention of the Holy See the fact that the absence of any form of public protest against the Nazi atrocities is endangering its moral prestige and undermining faith in the Church as well as in the person of the Holy Father. But all requests for intervention, he adds, have failed to produce results.

. . .

WE'RE MOVING to a new house. It's July and the heat seems to be expanding outward between the gray of the buildings and the noises rising up from the street. The war has made some changes in our lives, though still not that many. There are no more fräuleins who so stubbornly cleaned out our ears with cotton. Their place has been taken by a Romanian lady who is supposed to continue teaching us German, but Signora Olteanu speaks to us more often and more willingly in French. Annemarie is married, and back in her hometown she has children with her same sky-blue eyes on whom she ties aprons trimmed with flowered borders. Her husband is on combat duty in some part of Europe.

The blackouts have made the city quiet in the evenings and shutters are closed at dusk to keep even a thread of light from signaling our presence to the enemy. In the apartment on the other side of the street the curtains no longer allow anyone to see in. I have forgotten the taste of chocolate and of the bananas that I loved so much to bite into at snack time, but I still don't know hunger. The Fiat 1100 with the red leather seats has methane tanks on the roof and Papa uses it only for work. The Astura is in the garage, out of commission. I have just taken my graduating exam after my fifth year of elementary school without anyone asking me to wear a "Little Italian" uniform, which I still don't own.

On this radiant July morning we are moving. It is a very important morning. The furniture has been taken away and the kitchen disassembled. Italia and Letizia have accompanied our household furnishings, hanging on to the running board of the truck. The naked walls with their peach-branch wallpaper show the scars of time; sounds are amplified in the emptiness. The whole house seems to vibrate as it takes in waves of heat and dust. In the middle of that heat and dust stands Signora Della Seta, holding a metal plate with a boiled sea bass on it for us children on this day of confusion. A fish that no one can imagine how hard it must have been for her to come by and that we will eat in our new house amid the smell of pines and the chirping of cicadas. The light breeze coming in through the wide-open windows makes her pleated silk skirt flutter just slightly and lifts a few gray hairs off her pale forehead. The features of her face are erased by the bright light of July, the touch of her hands and the timber of her voice are lost in the great silence that surrounds her. This is the last time I will see her, and I rest my lips on her wrinkled cheek.

Nobody knows yet how great a question will envelop that mute image of Signora Della Seta as she hands us the fish, lying there among sprigs of green parsley. Her image dissolves on that July morning, leaving its mark on my memory as if silk-screened onto fabric. But it will never again be possible to find the living body that intercepted the sunlight or to capture the movement she made when she sat down in our living room, the rustling of her skirt. There is only that boiled sea bass, only that, devoured in just a few bites, its little white eye left on the plate.

AFTER WE GO excitedly from room to room amid the new smell of sun-yellowed grass, we open the crates and pull out the plates, the broom, and the mirror, the fetishes we have brought with us to this new house where the pine trees seem to be overflowing into the still-immaculate rooms. And in a seemingly never-ending sunset, hot, enervating, we lean out over the terrace to look at one of the workmen who built the house watering his victory garden. We who are used to the noisy grayness of via Flaminia are a little stunned by this new horizon of pines and cicadas, of white pigeons rising up in flight on the other side of the walls surrounding a convent. The man is drawing water in an old paint can, dripping it into a brick trough that horses once drank from. Two little boys with patches on their pants help him empty it between the rows of tomato plants. We watch them, trying to find points of conjunction, like two fingers reaching out to touch each other, some contact with everything that is new and different and that must from now on become familiar. We are blind, insensitive to the true significance of this endless day.

Without our suspecting it, the figure left behind to watch over nothing in the empty house is insinuating itself into our memory with its metal plate, its pleated silk skirt. Its tenacious, irresistible presence poses its question even today, with no possible response: Why her? Why that terrible journey toward death? Why didn't she seek safety sooner and relieve us of this unbearable burden, we Roman apostolic Catholics, baptized in Saint Peter's, raised in the love of Christ, in the memory of his Passion?

What can possibly be in the heads of those silly not-so-little girls (I'm eleven years old, my oldest sister is about to turn fourteen) who have just moved houses and on that July evening are preening like film stars in front of their dressing tables, each in her own new room with the light wood furniture designed by a fashionable architect. What do we ask from God, assuming that God is listening to us that summer, when we go to Mass the next Sunday at the Church of San Bellarmino? We offer an example of a model family as we follow in the missal, together with Papa and Mama, the Epistle of Saint Peter: "Friends, stand united, be compassionate, be moved by brotherly love, be merciful, modest, and humble. . . . Because the eyes of the Lord turn to the just and his ears to their prayers. . . . And if you will have suffered for jus-

tice you shall be blessed. Do not be afraid nor let your-
selves be disturbed by those who mistreat you." Later,
sitting in the pews, we listen to the sermon that, with
few variations, repeats the same concepts, the same
exhortations that defend themselves, as if armored,
against all personal involvement. Words that float upward
into the blue and gold mosaic vault like fish in an aquar-
ium, until they come to rest at the top, lost in absolute
boredom.

IN AUGUST of that interminable year of 1942, Ger-
hard Riegner, the representative of the World Jewish
Congress in Switzerland, sends to New York, through the
American ambassador in Bern, a new document on the
Final Solution. Another attempt is made to persuade
the pope to take a public position but nothing can break
the implacable silence of Pius XII. Also in August, Kurt
Gerstein, an officer who has managed to infiltrate the
highest levels of the SS, brings a detailed and chilling
report on what is happening at Auschwitz, which he has
seen with his own eyes. He goes to the nunciature in
Berlin and asks to be received by Monsignor Orsenigo.
But on learning that the person waiting to see him is a
military officer, the nuncio sends word that he will not be
able to receive him. Colonel Gerstein then gives his report
to the legal counsel of the archbishop of Berlin, asking

that it be transmitted to the Vatican. Archbishop Konrad von Preysing carries out the charge with dispatch.

That August during the pope's vacation at Castel Gandolfo, Mother Pasqualina tells us in her memoirs, he writes a very strong statement to be published in *L'Osservatore Romano,* an anguished protest denouncing the Nazi atrocities. But on hearing the news that in reprisal for public statements by Dutch bishops, the Germans have sent forty thousand Jews to the gas chambers, the pope burns the pages in the great kitchen fireplace. Mother Pasqualina describes Pius XII as looking terribly pale as the flames devour the pages. What was written on those pages has never been discovered and Pius XII left no trace of them. But the first question that comes to mind is, "Did Pius XII therefore know in August 1942 about the Final Solution and the gas chambers?" If we are to judge from Mother Pasqualina's memoirs, the answer is yes.

Documents published in recent years report the same events regarding the Dutch bishops in a completely different light. On July 11, on receiving news that the Jews are about to be deported, the Dutch Catholic bishops send a telegram to Arthur Seyss-Inquart, Reich commissioner for the Netherlands: "Dismayed by the measures that have been taken in Holland against the Jews, excluding them from the community, the churches here represented have now learned with profound horror of the new measures condemning men, women, and children to deportation to Germany or to countries currently under German control. The suffering thus caused the tens of thousands of people, the certainty that these measures offend the most profound moral sense of the Dutch people, their opposition to the laws of God with regard to justice and mercy, compel us to address a most pressing appeal that these measures not be implemented. Furthermore, given that they affect Christians of Jewish origin, our appeal becomes all the more insistent, because this decision excludes them from the life of the Church." On July 14, Governor Seyss-Inquart's assistant, Schmidt, sends for Pastor Dijckmeester, interim secretary of the General Synod of Bishops, and informs him that Jews converted to Christianity before 1941 (a total of about 1,500 Catholics and Protestants) will not be deported. Dijckmeester thanks him but deplores the fact that this provision does not include all Jews, baptized or not. Immediately thereafter, Catholics and Protestants meet together and draft a letter to be read in churches on Sunday, July 26, along with the telegram to Seyss-Inquart. Informed of this joint letter, Seyss-Inquart sends for Dijckmeester and prohibits him from mentioning the telegram and from making public the results of their meeting; the agreement, he insists, must remain secret. On the twenty-fourth the General Synod declares itself in favor of the agreement. Catholic priests, however, read the letter in church as previously agreed, mentioning the telegram. On August 2, Schmidt, in a speech reported in the newspapers the following day, declares that if the Catholic clergy fail to respect the agreement, the government will be obliged to treat Catholic Jews as its worst enemies and to deport them immediately to the East.

The almost seven hundred Jewish Protestants are saved—for the moment.

AFTER the hard work of moving, we leave, as we do every year, for our summer vacation. It is a shorter vacation than usual, though. Flaminia and her parents aren't so much in fashion anymore; maybe political issues have started to weigh a bit too heavily. We're in Rapallo and the *zampirone* is burning on the windowsill to keep away the mosquitoes that fly up from the canal at night. The evenings are dark but the moon and the stars reflect off the sea and light up the beach, silhouetting the palm trees and the children running all around. We go for a walk. My sisters and I now part of a small group of friends and every evening we walk along the waterfront until the road starts to curve and vanishes into a garden thick with trees. Sometimes we sing songs like "Giarabub" and "Quel mazzolin di fiori" (That Little Bunch of Flowers) or children's songs. At the cinema they're showing *Suss l'ebreo* (The Jew

Suss). The poster shows the Jew with filthy clothes and a hook nose, "skin the greenish color of swamp mud," as Giovanni Papini puts it. None of us goes to see it. A couple of afternoons we rent bicycles and pedal along the road toward Santa Margherita, where we stop to eat a snack in the shade of the chestnut trees, mostly pears and grapes. Behind us on her bicycle Signorina Giampietro, responsible for our safety, struggles to keep up. We are tired of fräuleins and governesses; breasts have begun to lift my big sisters' shirts and we want to be free. So we throw her off our trail. She looks for us, calling each of our names in turn. We hide our bicycles in the shadows of the chestnut trees and have fun watching her pedal back and forth, all sweaty, the rare passing cars honking at her from behind.

ON AUGUST 14 *L'Osservatore Romano* remembers Father Kolbe, the Polish priest who died at Auschwitz, in its own way. "Father Kolbe," the paper reports, "silently disappeared one year ago."

Effective October 1, Jews in territories under the jurisdiction of the Reich are no longer entitled to fresh meat, salted meat, eggs, wheat products, milk, vegetables, legumes, or fruit. Instead they are each allowed half a kilo of turnips a week.

On October 8 Archbishop Preysing of Berlin protests in church against the persecution of the clergy. Many priests have been deported, he says, seminaries and convents shut down, a number of churches closed to worship. Catholic schools, too, have been closed and crucifixes taken down from where they had hung for centuries. But his protest remains confined within his diocese, a voiceless sound without resonance or echo.

On November 8 the Americans, under the command of General Dwight D. Eisenhower, land in North Africa and the Germans, to prevent solidarity between the French there and on the other side of the Mediterranean, occupy the part of France that until then had enjoyed a kind of pseudo-independence. A small part of the newly occupied territory, from the Alps to the Côte d'Azur, is assigned to Italy. In the zone occupied by the troops of the Reich, whose methods have been perfected by now, the roundup of all Jews begins immediately. To escape deportation, thousands of the persecuted, thanks to the well-disposed local authorities, find refuge in the tiny strip of land that is Italy's. In a short time the number of Jews there grows from twenty thousand to almost fifty thousand. On July 21, 1943, one of the commanders in chief of the SS in France will complain to Berlin: "The attitude of the Italians is and has been incomprehensible. The Italian authorities and the Italian police are protecting the Jews with all means in their power. The Italian influence zone, particularly the Côte d'Azur, has become the promised land for Jews resident in France."

In his Christmas message for 1942, Pius XII mentions for the first time the catastrophe that has struck the Jews. It is the subject of a few lines on the twenty-fourth page of a twenty-six-page speech: "Mankind owes these vows to those hundreds of thousands of people who, through no fault of their own but sometimes solely because of their nationality or race, are destined for death or gradual extinction." The speech then drops the question of race, never to return to it. Instead Pius XII continues, "Mankind owes these vows to those thousands and thousands of noncombatants, women, children, the sick, the old, whom the air war, whose horrors we have already denounced many times, has, without distinction, deprived of their lives, their property, their health, their homes, and places of charitable and religious asylum . . ."

OUTSIDE IT IS RAINING and we're in the sitting room on the ground floor of a hotel pompously and inappropriately named the Grand Hotel Brusson, in a vacation resort no more beautiful or famous than many others. It's the summer of 1943. Hunger has barreled its way into our daily lives. I no longer have shoes and instead wear clogs like the local farmers. I've grown and my clothes are all short and tight on me; the weather is dark, it's cold, and the euphoria over the fall of Mussolini on July 24, voted out of office after the Allied landing in Sicily, ended a while ago. To pass the time while it rains, a bunch of us are playing at acting out films. One of the group is a boy named Emanuele Muggia. I don't know where he's from or why he's there. Maybe he's in love with my sister Teresa. I'm almost sure that's it—all the boys fall in love with her sooner or later. Emanuele Muggia is Jewish and I don't like his touchiness, his always being so defensive. I don't like him. But I'm little and don't count for very much. I'm awkward, and a cumbersome appliance for straightening my teeth makes me hiss when I talk. Another member of the group is Giorgia Boagno; he's seventeen and a short time later he'll decide to join the Nazi- and Fascist-controlled area of northern Italy, the Social Republic. And there's Paolo Spraiano, who everybody calls Pillo. He's cocky and he's got a thick head of curly hair. His girlfriend is the cutest girl even though he's shabbily dressed and all that remain of his tennis shoes are the top halves. Paolo will make the opposite choice from Giorgio Boagno's, joing the anti-Nazi liberation forces, and a decisive factor will be his seeing Primo Levi carried away in chains from the mountains above Brusson.

But all of this is yet to happen; we are still in limbo. Only Emanuele is closer to hell. My sister goes over to him and grasps the corner of one of the lapels of his jacket, then gives him a provocative look and squeezes the material between her fingers until it looks like a pig's ear. She doesn't realize that her gesture is offensive, insulting to a Jew. There, it looks just like the little ear of a baby pig. She laughs. It takes only an instant: the crisp noise of the slap across her face bursts into our little universe like a fireball. Before anyone can even open his mouth Emanuele has left the room, slamming the door behind him. My sister's eyes are full of tears as she walks around the room, a dismayed look on her face. One of the boys starts to giggle. Maybe he's the one who put her up to that cruel, mocking gesture, saying to her, "Come on, do it, it's only a joke."

WE LEAVE BRUSSON for the countryside of Monferrato, crammed into a bus that's like a chicken coop. Then we get on a train where the only place for us is in the freight car and we girls sit on the floor with our feet dangling over the side. It takes a whole day to go just over a hundred kilometers. It's still hot on the plains, still summer, and we're having fun looking out from that unusual position. The stations go by slowly, one after another, and at a certain point while we are stopped at a platform, I don't remember where, a train passes us, rattling speedily down the rails; it's the royal train carrying the princess of Piedmont back to Rome with the little princes.

September is full of light. A hot, oblique sun ripens the grapes hanging in rows on the hillsides, warms the old green door of the house. After the hunger we have white bread again, butter and milk. Our bicycles have been brought down out of the attic and we pedal all around on the dusty back roads between the fields where the corn is high, splash around in our bare feet in the water of the drainage ditches under the rows of poplar trees, chase after toads that jump through our fingers, laugh at the silliest things. The new government's armistice with the Allies is just around the corner but we don't know that and the days seem to us like the first of a long season.

Then on September 8, the news hits us like a rock and out of our peaceful summer comes a swarm of voices, memories, frantic comings and goings, hope and fear, euphoria and aimlessness. The next morning a boy, one of our guests, gets on the first bus to town to report to the military district of Alessandria; in the absence of clear orders, his call-up from the draft board may still be valid. At eleven o'clock, in the crossfire of conflicting reports about whether Italy will fight against Gemany or not, the general happiness suffers its first blow. At one o'clock, when we see our unlucky guest come walking back up the road, sweaty and exhausted, we know the news is bad. He has nothing left from his suitcase but his toothbrush and he has come more than twenty kilometers on foot after a boat providentially ferried him across the Tanaro. The Germans have invaded Italy and in Alessandria they have set up checkpoints on all the bridges and are arresting anyone wearing a uniform; for the time being, all Italian soldiers are barricaded inside the citadel.

Later some fleeing soldiers come to the house asking for clothes so they can take off their uniforms and go back home. And when rumors start to spread that the Germans are on their way to our area, I pack up a bundle with my diary and my tennis shoes, my most precious possessions, and put a package of sanitary napkins inside. They, too, though not quite as much as the tennis shoes, have their own specific value. At sunset two Germans on a motorcycle with a sidecar rumble by and, without even stopping, vanish down the road to Occimano. A little disappointed I unpack the bundle but Papa gives the order to prepare for an immediate return to Rome. The Allies have landed at Salerno and he is sure that they will be in Rome in just a few days (actually it will take more than nine months). Mama, with help from Italia and Letizia, has started filling one suitcase with pears and another with walnuts; she has had them wrap up the eggs and chickens. The shipper comes to pick up our trunks. But my brother doesn't want to go back to Rome; he says we'll all die of hunger there.

The next morning he goes to the station in Giarole to prevent our trunks from being shipped. He takes his new bicycle, a silver Wolsitt, and disappears into the hills toward Mosa. Sitting on the steps of the house we crack open one last walnut with a sudden feeling of insecurity. We're surrounded by footsteps, the thumping of carpet beaters, orders and counterorders. And all of a sudden Papa's anger explodes, cold, precise like the wrath of God that sees all, knows all, and punishes. I get a slap in the face (the second of my life) because I refuse to be a spy and tell where my brother is hiding. I don't cry. Our plans do not change—we will be leaving that same night. And before evening my brother is back home again, hungry and covered with dust. The grapes in the vineyards have already been harvested and the farmers are all barricaded inside their houses. He hasn't eaten since morning.

(My brother will run away again, to enlist in the army of national liberation, which fought the Nazis and Fascists occupying the north of the country. That time, too, he'll come back all wet and defeated the same evening, cold and hungry, after a day of frantic searching by my parents. The family will go on joking a long while about this second failed attempt, about the hero who never manages to act heroically. But with the passage of time the event has taken on a different meaning and to me it now seems like the only magnanimous effort to take part in the common suffering and fatigue, common in the sense of being everybody's. An attempt, though bumbling and inept, to break out of the protective family circle, where values, ideas, feelings are processed and resolved only among ourselves. He was the only one of us who felt the impulse to put himself on the line. He tried, closing the door silently behind him as the rain poured outside and you couldn't even tell if it was day or night. This time he had some bread and salami in his pocket, but that didn't change anything.)

A little carriage called a *berlina* takes us to Giarole to catch one of the last trains and avoid being machine-gunned. We look out anxiously through the worn, yellowed curtains at the deserted countryside bathed in the light of the sunset against the distant profile of the Alps. I don't remember the journey to Rome anymore. I just remember the uninterrupted sight of houses in shambles, rooms broken open like rotten apples with their wallpaper showing, sometimes with a painting still hanging crooked on the wall, a sink, the hood of a stove. I remember a venerable old railroad car whose compartment doors opened inward. The endless station stops, the railroad cars reduced to rubble or turned upside down amid piles of torn-up rails, the wait for the spasmodic lurch of the locomotive to pull the train forward again. The coal smoke that turned our nostrils black, our blackened fingers hanging on to the window to see outside, my blackened shirt collar and handkerchief.

. . .

IN ROME the Germans are everywhere. On October 10, after a shoot-out at Saint Paul's Gate sees a few desperate soldiers and their officers die in defense of their city, General Rainer Stahel takes charge. That same day, Pius XII sends Ernst von Weizsäcker, who had replaced Diego von Bergen as German ambassador a few months earlier, a document requesting that the autonomy of Vatican City be respected and asking what measures will be taken to ensure its security. A second document follows immediately declaring that the Vatican had no part in the negotiations for the armistice.

We learn that in Mirabello the two Germans on the motorcycle came back, and with them an entire command that has installed itself in our house. In the big double bed in my mother's room there now sleeps a captain of the Wehrmacht and his young mistress. I am very worried because in my diary, which I forgot on top of the wardrobe, I had written "M Mussolini"—Down with Mussolini.

Even the cloistered convent on via Salaria has been requisitioned, and in the garden, where in July we were still able to hear the bells play the Angelus, German soldiers in shirtsleeves cut wood and pigeons hop around undisturbed in the rows of lettuce left abandoned in the frantic escape. At dusk, melancholy sentinels venture occasional compliments to the women who pass hurriedly in front of the austere black main gate. We are back at school. October 16, an infamous date, is our second day.

It's the concierge who informs Papa: the Levi family was taken away by the SS that morning at six. As for the Della Seta family, Domenico knows nothing. They left the house a few days ago without telling anybody.

But the Levis and Della Setas have already become pale memories and my attention is concentrated on what my mother is telling me about a woman who had just given birth when, still in her nightgown, she had been forced by the SS to climb onto a truck and who in the confusion of the orders and the screaming, had thrown her baby in its swaddling clothes into the arms of an astonished and frightened passerby. As my mother is talking I can see that woman, desperate and unkempt, just as she must have looked to the eyes of those who had been passing by and watched, petrified.

IN THE 1938 CENSUS there were some 12,000 Roman Jews (the census lists showing a total of 13,376 "persons of Jewish race" included the entire province). It's difficult to know how many of those people are still there in October 1943 and how many others have come down from the German-occupied north in the hope that Rome will be safer. At dawn on October 16 the Germans succeed in rounding up 1,259 Jews. It is a Saturday (the Germans always choose Saturday because they know it will be easier to find families together) and at four o'clock in the morning they begin shooting in the streets of the ghetto to prevent people from leaving their houses. It is all done very quickly. Awakened by heavy pounding on their doors, men, women, and children are given twenty minutes to get dressed and pack food for eight days, throw their things into a suitcase, and take all the money they have in the house (money that the Germans will swiftly arrange to take from them, down to the last lira). The lightening-fast operation is carried out by 365 SS men just arrived the night before under the command of Theodor Dannecker, who in the first days of October had set himself up in a modest hotel in via Po. Of the 1,259 deportees some 237 will be released that evening because they are non-Jews, Aryan spouses, or children of mixed marriages or because they are citizens of neutral countries. Of the 1,023 deportees of October 16, only 17 will return. (The 1,023rd, Costanza Calò Sermoneta, was not home when her family was arrested and ran desperately to Termini Station, where she asked and was permitted to climb aboard the car that was carrying her husband and children.) To these deportees must also be added another 723 Jews arrested in Rome during the subsequent eight months of German occupation. Of these, 75 will be executed at the Ardeatine Caves and four at the interment camp in Fòssoli. The remaining 644 will be, like the others, deported to Auschwitz.

The roundup operation is carried out right in front of the pope, as it were, just a few hundred meters from Saint Peter's. There is considerable agitation in the Vatican. Secretary of State Luigi Maglione summons Ambassador Weizsäcker. The tone of the meeting is quite friendly, and after listening to Monsignor Maglione's protest the ambassador asks, "How do you think the Holy See would react if things were to continue?" The answer couldn't be more diplomatic: "The Holy See would prefer not to be put in the position of having to voice its disapproval."

In his book on Italian Jews under Fascism, Renzo De Felice gives the following account of October 16:

As soon as the Holy See got word of the roundup it arranged for two semiofficial contacts to be made with the Germans, one by Monsignor Hudal, rector of Santa Maria dell'Anima, and the other by Father Pfeiffer, of the Order of the Divine Savior, having them note—as demonstrated by Monsignor Hudal's letter to General Stahel, the military commandant in Rome [General Stahel was a practicing Catholic from Bavaria, as was Father Pfeiffer]—that in the interest of peaceful relations between the Vatican and the

German military command it was opportune that the arrests be stopped immediately, and making it understood that it was not to be ruled out that the pope might take an official position against the arrests. According to a document of P. Duclos, the two contacts achieved the desired result: on October 17 Monsignor Hudal was informed by the German commandant in Rome that Himmler, on hearing of the position taken by the Vatican, had given instructions to suspend the arrests. To the great surprise of the Nazis, Pope Pius XII had absolutely no desire to go beyond these two semiofficial contacts. On October 17 Ambassador Weizsäcker, reporting to Berlin of the consternation in the Vatican provoked by the events of the day before and giving his account of the pressures that were being brought to bear on the pope to break his silence, did not exclude the possibility that Pius XII could be induced to take an official position. On October 28, however, Weizsäcker was able definitively to reassure the foreign minister in Berlin: "Although under pressure from many sources, the pope has not let himself be pushed into demonstrating any disapproval of the deportation of the Jews from Rome."

The only official reaction is a rather insipid comment published in *L'Osservatore Romano* on October 25–26, a few days after most of the Jews deported from Rome had already died in the gas chambers at Auschwitz-Birkenau. In contorted and confused prose, the newspaper emphasizes that the pope extends to everyone the benefit of his paternal solicitude, regardless of nationality, race, or religion, and that the manifold and ceaseless activities of Pius XII have been further increased in recent times, due to the ever-greater suffering of so many unfortunate people.

Although there were no other roundups like the one on October 16, the daily systematic hunt for Jews in Rome continues, resulting in the additional 723 arrests. The operation is partly organized, in this second phase, by the Germans but above all by the Italian police headquarters in Rome.

Religious institutions left free to welcome anyone who is in danger generously take in adults as well as children, whether baptized or not. In Rome alone some one hundred convents and fifty-five monasteries take people in. Food and clothing are provided by way of the Vatican for those in need. And although it is true that the war is going in such a way as to make a German defeat in the not-too-distant future seem more and more probable (a consideration that tips the balance in favor of the persecuted, the potential avengers of tomorrow), it is also true that the prospect of defeat makes the Germans, if possible, even more ferocious. The risks involved in helping Jews are very real. In a raid conducted in the middle of the night of February 3–4, 1944, the Fascist police force open the doors of the Benedictine convent next to Saint Paul's Basilica and arrest sixty-four people, nine of whom are Jews. Although there are no other such incidents, it is certain that the religious who choose to give asylum to their very dangerous guests must live in more or less constant fear that something similar will happen.

Fortunately for them, the Germans already have more than enough to do to maintain order in Rome without risking diplomatic incidents with the Vatican. And until the Allies' arrival there is no serious attempt on the part of the Germans to go in and take Jews out of the convents. No one else is arrested or deported for taking Jews in, as they are, however, in other countries under Nazi regimes. And for the duration of the occupation, automobiles with Vatican license plates circulate freely and in total safety while the German sentinels requested by Pius XII watch over the security of the minuscule state.

In *Memory Fields,* Shlomo Breznitz, who was a child in Czechoslovakia during the war and whose parents, who later died in Auschwitz, arranged for him to be taken in by an orphanage run by nuns in a small town near Bratislava, tells how in April 1945 the Germans came to the convent to take him away and how the nuns hid him under a mattress in the infirmary. Unable to find him, the Germans, sure that he was hidden there, came back a short time later with bloodhounds, but the mother superior stood in front of the door yelling at them. Many years later Breznitz, by now an adult, returned to the convent to find out what it was the mother superior had yelled that had kept the Germans from coming in to get him. But the mother superior had died and none of the other sisters was able to tell him anything, and maybe nobody ever knew the words she had yelled. All they remembered was that she had stood in front of the door to block them from coming in and that she had yelled and yelled without paying any attention to the dogs growling back at her, ready to jump. "The fascination of hiding doesn't amount to much," Breznitz writes, "compared to the mystery of courage, especially courage on behalf of others. It is when fear tells you to run away and your mind tells you to stay, when your body tells you to save yourself and your soul to save others, that courage goes to battle with fear, its eternal companion."

ONCE THE deportations are a reality, why do the Levis fail to take steps to save themselves in time?

The ferocious cunning of the German command certainly has more than a secondary role in their misfortune. On September 26, 1943, Herbert Kappler, the SS commander in Rome, demands that the Jewish community hand over fifty kilograms of gold, lest he proceed with the immediate deportation of two hundred Jews. With great sacrifice, people who have already been squeezed in every conceivable way by the racial laws and by the suffering of war manage to put together the fifty kilos, some of which is contributed by "Aryans" who show up at the synagogue where the gold is being collected to offer a ring, a necklace, or a bracelet. (Pius XII offers to make a loan of twelve kilos that the Jewish community can give back at a later date. But there is no need.) The dastardly and shameful fraud of the gold ransom that fails to buy the Jews' freedom seems too much even for the Germans. Everyone expects cruelty, but not the failure to keep their word. The Nazis have presented themselves as the emblem of order that is blind and absurd but order nevertheless, and they are renowned for the ruthlessness with which they demand that rules be respected. Disobeying the injunction requiring Jews to declare any change of domicile can be more dangerous than seeking precarious refuge somewhere in the city. And whether they are small storeowners in the ghetto or members of the upper class, Rome's Jews respect the concept of legality. In the few decades since the unification of Italy, rather than losing force, this concept has become even stronger in response to the pressure on Jews to demonstrate their professional ethics. Yet the small storeowners who owe their economic survival to respect for the rules in their relations with their clients are among the largest group of victims.

To save yourself you need an extra dose of cunning, which the Levis don't have.

SOMETIMES I think that the Levi's lack of cunning was not the only reason for their destruction. I think about us and about our house looking out on the pine trees in the evening silence, the orchard abandoned by the nuns where we watch the Germans splitting wood. About my father who in September of 1943 closes his office rather than collaborate with the Germans and spends his afternoons in one of my mother's old bathrobes, covering pages and pages of postage stamps with talcum powder. It is as good a way as any of trying to protect part of the family savings, which inflation is steadily eating away. Even we girls, once the curfew sounds, are called in to help, and those wavy-edged sheets accumulate in piles on the table, the image of our king, now a deserter in Brindisi, repeating itself, amid clouds of talcum, into infinity: light green, brown, reddish purple.

For nine months we wait for the phantom soldiers, so near and yet so far, the English, Americans, South Africans, Moroccans, Poles, Canadians who keep sending reassuring messages over the airwaves encoded in child's talk: "The pasta is done," "Luigi has lost his notebook," "The apples are ripe." On clear days we can hear, blown by the southern wind, the intermittent dull booming of their cannons, sunk in the mud in the coastal swamps south of Rome.

Papa wants me to practice piano at least half an hour every afternoon before going out to play in the fields below the house. I put an open book above the keys and for the entire half hour, as my hands move up and down the keyboard over the same set of notes, I turn one page after another of a novel without ever taking my eyes off it, probably without understanding any of it. Just to assert my independence. As soon as I finish I scramble down the stairs to meet my friends.

For me it is an enjoyable time, even though my stomach is almost always unsatisfied and my hands are itchy with chilblains. For fear of bombings the nuns send us home from school in midmorning and my mother spends her days trying to pull off the miracle of the loaves and fishes, driven by our voracious, insatiable hunger. Signora Olteanu is still with us but the difficulties of moving from one area of the city to another have reduced her visits to two afternoons a week, during which, right after lunch, she takes me for a walk on via Salaria. We speak in French, a language she likes much more than German, and as we walk along the city wall in via Savoia where Nazi Field Marshal Albert Kesselring's

gang sends to their deaths anyone who refuses to serve
the Social Republic, she tells me about her youth. We
walk and walk, her resolute old-girl step sounding in the
semideserted street below the peeling plaster of the high
walls. We pass the rusted gates, now always closed, and
for the brief space of a walk she forgets the hunger and
the humiliation, the anguish for her children lost in
some part of Europe. And as via Salaria loses itself in the
tangle of desolate pathways winding to the Aniene
River, from under the turban that keeps sliding down
around her thinned-out face her eyes sparkle with memories of grand and sublime emotions, of tunes played
on the piano, and of sunsets on the Black Sea, so fiery
and sweet.

In the other areas of my life, I have finally been set free.
I can go without washing myself or combing my hair, can
run around right up until the curfew sounds or read for
hours curled up in a chair. I even stop undressing when I
go to bed, sliding my pajamas on over my slip without
even taking my kneesocks off, so that the next morning
I can get up at the last minute and be ready to go, book
bag in hand, in three minutes. In the evenings, on our
knees in Mama's room, the family gathers together to
recite the rosary, the talcum powder still hovering in the
air, clinging to our clothes, our hair, to the soles of our
shoes. I am so tired I can't keep my eyes from closing as
the joyful, painful, and glorious words go by one by

one in the profound silence that comes with the night. The rare screech of a passing car is heard, the double thump of a loose sewer cover, the whistle of a faraway train.

WHAT DID they expect from us, the Della Setas, engineer Levi, and that boy who loved to play Chopin? Didn't they understand that the inconceivable became real because it concerned, fatally, only *them*? They were guilty without guilt. They should have known that the Vatican's diplomatic maneuvers to persuade the Germans to give up some of their human booty favored those who had owned up to the deicide, those who had washed away their guilt by bending their heads under the waters of baptism. The Jews who stubbornly refused to convert would sooner or later become victims of their pride and perseverance in error. A painful and ineluctable destiny separated them from *us*.

In the street there are those who turn away from the Jews with stolid indifference and there are those who betray them for five thousand lire, the price the Germans pay for every adult Jewish man reported to them (the price goes down to three thousand lire for women and a thousand for children). But there are also those who don't think twice about risking their own lives to save them.

I know some wonderful stories of people who hid entire families, sharing for months the miserable amounts of food available from the rationing program and feeling their blood freeze at every unexpected ring of the doorbell. Mirella Calò was a four-year-old girl with three slightly older sisters. On the afternoon of October 15, 1943, a neighborhood street singer, Romolo Balzani, warned her father he had heard talk at the police station that the Germans were planning to come that night to take away the Jews. Her father lowered the shutter of his spare auto parts store in via del Pellegrino and ran to his house in the Testaccio neighborhood. He didn't have a phone so he passed the word as best he could to some of his relatives. His wife dressed their daughters in two pairs of underpants, several sweaters, one on top of the other, and coats and left the house. It was already late, the streets were emptying, and so, unable to think of anything better, Mirella's father took all five of them to the whorehouse in via del Pellegrino where the madam had said she would be willing to hide them for a night. Then he tried to save himself by heading for the country.

Mirella and her mother and three sisters stayed in the basement of that whorehouse for eight months. They went out into the courtyard only in the evening after the curfew. When all the clients had left, the Signora or Signor Adolfo would come down to give them something to eat. During the day in the basement one couldn't talk or make the least little noise because of the constant traffic of men, including German soldiers, up and down the stairs. Every so often, to distract those four girls condemned to silence, Signor Adolfo would come down to play cards. So four-year-old Mirella Calò learned how to play "three sevens," *mariaccia, briscola,* and *scopone.*

Mirella's aunt Elisabetta also lived in Testaccio. Warned by her brother-in-law, she went out to the street just as she was, with her three children and her purse. The curfew was about to start and in a fit of panic she had them all climb into a taxi. When the driver turned around to ask her where she wanted to go she answered, "I don't know. I'm Jewish and the Germans are coming to get us." The taxi driver turned white. Holy Madonna, what am I going to do with these people? he must have thought. But after a moment of shock during which they sat there staring at one another, each more scared than the other, the man began to drive and took all four of them to his house, where he lived with his wife and two children. And they stayed there for eight months as well, on top of one another in two rooms, fed with the little extra food that Ermete, the taxi driver, and his wife managed to put together.

In via degli Scipioni, on the corner of via Leone IV, where the street changes character from upper-middle-class houses with gardens and orange trees to storefronts and late-nineteenth-century apartment buildings, there is one of those buildings with several entrances. Number 35 was the home of the Sermoneta family: father, mother, grandfather, and seventeen-year-old Rosetta. On the morning of October 16, at seven o'clock, the concierge came to their front door with two SS officers. As the four of them were getting dressed, trying to put on as many heavy things as possible, one of the SS men, having cut the phone wires, punctured the tires of their bicycles, and assured himself that everything was going smoothly, went on his way. Rosetta's mother had time to pack her best linens in a suitcase and give it to the displaced persons who lived in the apartment next door. Then, in front of the remaining SS man, his rifle at the ready, the four of them went down to the foyer with what little luggage they were able to carry.

The truck hadn't arrived yet, the air was cold, and it was drizzling. Some of the food stores already had their shutters rolled up and a small line was forming in front of the greengrocer's. Rosetta was given permission to go as far as the bakery on the corner to get some bread. When she came back to where her parents and grandfather were waiting in the front doorway, a small group had formed near them, passersby who had observed the three people standing there with their suitcases under the eye of an SS man, his rifle leveled at them. It wasn't hard to understand what was going on. Everyone in via degli Scipioni knew the Sermonetas. Rosetta had been

born in that house and, until the racial laws had separated them, she had walked to school every morning
with the baker's daughter.

The truck was late, and after a quarter of an hour the
group had grown. The SS man finally pushed the Sermonetas into the street and had them turn the corner into
via Leone IV, hoping to see the truck arrive. The group
followed them, and as the German soldier kept pushing
the Sermonetas ahead with their suitcases, it became
larger and began to move closer and closer. Behind the
family the now-compact group crossed viale Giulio
Cesare and turned onto viale Milizie under the tall
beech trees with their yellow autumn leaves. More
people joined and some started shouting, "Come on, run
for it," but the Sermonetas couldn't find the courage. All
of a sudden a young girl grabbed Rosetta by the sleeve;
she was the daughter of the woman who had the fruit
stand on viale Giulio Cesare. She pulled Rosetta inside
an entryway on the other side of the street, but the
frightened concierge sent them away, saying, "No, no,
not here." Meanwhile the small anonymous crowd had
closed around the SS man, as Rosetta's mother left her
suitcase on the ground and slipped off the heavy overcoat that hindered her movements. In an instant, father,
mother, daughter, and grandfather were down the first
street on the left, then right onto via Giovanni Bettolo,
where they went in the first doorway they came to. They

were going down into the basement when they were called back up: a taxi with its motor running was waiting for them in the street. They never knew who had called it or where it came from; the Sermonetas were too frightened to ask questions. Rosetta's father gave the address of his barber, who had told him some time ago that he'd be willing to help him out.

Rosetta and her mother stayed at the barber's house in piazza di Lucina for a couple of days while her father and grandfather stayed with the pastor of the Church of Santa Maria Liberatrice. After that the four of them, separately, moved from refuge to refuge, with Rosetta living for several months in a convent of the Sisters of Charity in piazza dei Quiriti, where the superior, Sister Marguerite Bèmes, had been hiding other Jews for some time. Today she is recognized by the State of Israel as one of the righteous Gentiles. (It was later known that the young SS soldier, in tears, went back to via degli Scipioni and rang at the apartment of the displaced persons next to the Sermonetas, causing pandemonium to break out. He wanted at all costs to take away at least the girl, who was more or less the same age as Rosetta.)

In Denmark the Germans were able to deport no more than 513 of the 5,600 Jews. Someone warned the victims in time and the Danes mobilized to take them to safety across the narrow stretch of water that separates Denmark from Sweden. Any vessel able to float was considered good enough. And Sweden welcomed them all, without limit.

THERE IS a black border around those guiltless days of ours. If the Levis did not defend themselves and were unable to imagine the inconceivable, surely it is not least because they considered themselves, like all other Romans, beneficiaries of certain guarantees. For too long they had shared with us happy days and sad, fears, cowardice, hopes. Going up and down the same stairs, drinking the same tea, stirring the spoon in the cup, they had spoken the same language, in the lexical sense but also in the emotional sense, for far too long to think of themselves as *other*. How to imagine the monstrous sense of isolation they must have felt in the grip of the SS and their orders, which, within twenty minutes, eliminated them from the human race?

Nobody summons the courage to stop Dannecker's men from thundering up the stairs in their boots at 21 via Flaminia and bursting into the Levis' apartment. Nobody stops the trucks that drive away loaded with men and women and children awakened so horribly from their sleep. Pius XII does not appear, white and solemn, at the Trastevere station to stand on the tracks in front of the convoy and block its departure, as he appeared among the crowd the day the San Lorenzo neighborhood was bombed. The cars are sealed shut and the train leaves without incident, the whistle of the locomotive blowing along via Salaria.

Pius XII stays closed behind the windows of his room, where the canaries Hansel and Gretel take off into the air on their brief flights. My father and mother, who surely must feel compassion for the Levis, do not forget, even that day, the sheets of stamps and the meat, and the bread, and the eggs. And on the evening of October 16, the student this writer once was, recites the rosary, sighing with boredom as she does every evening, letting her eyelids droop amid the singsong of the Hail Marys and Our Fathers. She does not give the slightest thought to supplicating her God, who after all is also the God of the Levis and the Della Setas, to send the avenging angel down to help them. She feels no impulse to scream, to do something for that boy with the cheerful face who used to ring their bell, his leather ball tucked tightly under his arm. No need to concern herself with the fate of the woman who came into the semidark room where a child lay, hot with fever in a big double bed. Signora Della Seta would sit down while my mother remained standing behind her, resting her arms on the back of the chair, both of them smiling, delighted to watch that child peer out from under the sheets to open her present.

On that night of October 16, the thoughts of that girl who was no longer little (by now five foot three and wearing size 8 shoes) aren't much different from usual, focused mainly on the notes she exchanges, by way of an elaborate system of pulleys and strings, with the Calcagno girls, who live in the apartment under hers.

I DON'T KNOW what happened to Emanuele Muggia after September 8, 1943. We never saw him again. When we left Brusson at the end of August, he was already gone. Fortunately his name is not included among those of the victims recorded in *Il libro della memoria* (The Book of Memory), by Liliana Picciotto Fargion, who has tried patiently to reconstruct the fates, at least in their essential points, of those Italians who were killed because they were members of the Hebrew race. I assume he was saved—or at least I hope so, because the list is unavoidable incomplete. But the story of Giorgio Levi is one I know well. By one of those unforeseen coincidences that suddenly opens up a piece of history I was able to hear it from a girl who was with him the morning they were deported, a sort of cousin-sibling because their mothers were sisters and their fathers brothers. Her name is Alberta and she was twenty-four years old then. She had just come to Rome from Ferrara with her family. A few days earlier a German soldier, accompanied by a Fascist police officer, had awakened them in the middle of the night, searching through their house, rifle pointed, for her grandfather, in whose name the telephone was listed. This is her account of that morning:

Uncle Mario, in a letter he sent after September 8, insisted that we come to Rome. He had met with Dante Almansi, the president of the Italian Jewish community, who had suggested he have his relatives from northern Italy come to Rome, under the illusion that Rome was an open city and that the Allies would reach there soon.

We arrived at the station in Ferrara on October 12 with only a few personal effects, so as not to look conspicuous. We didn't have a suitcase; our handbags were stuffed with underwear and we each had a winter coat over our arms with a dress or two or a sweater stuffed up the sleeves and fastened inside with a pin so we wouldn't lose them. . . . Our aunt and uncle's apartment wasn't very big, so we decided that my father would spend the nights in a pension run by Signora Mortara in piazza Fiume. Giorgio and I made up a double bed for my mother, my sister, Piera, and me in his room; he fixed himself up in the maid's room. Piera and I immediately started looking for jobs. At first we gave private lessons but what we really wanted were live-in jobs that, even if they didn't pay money, would solve the problem of finding enough for us to eat without ration stamps. We also thought that if we split up it would be easier for us to blend in. At dinner on the fifteenth we reported on our efforts. . . . I had found a woman, a friend of a friend, who was bedridden with phlebitis and was happy to have me as a live-in maid. . . . Aunt Alba, who was usually quite pessimistic, was all animated and hopeful. She had gone to see a friend of hers that afternoon to wish her well on her patron saint's day and to offer her house during the day as a hideout for the woman's son, an officer who had stopped wearing his uniform on September 8. He was only worried about having a place during the day because at night there was the curfew and nobody went out anyway. I listened in dismay. Then when I reported on the results of my search, I was even more upset. Aunt Alba was not to be moved: "As long as we have this house, you're not going to be anybody's maid. You'll give your private lessons."

I mention these things to give an idea of the illusions that so many people were still clinging to as of October 15, 1943. The Jews feared only for the men, so in the mornings Uncle Mario left the house right after the curfew ended and wandered around the city as long as possible. After all, it wouldn't be long before the Allies got there. I remember that dinner, out last dinner. Aunt Alba, always a health nut, counted the calories we had consumed and decided we each had to eat a walnut to bring us up to the necessary amount. I remember Giorgio at the piano playing a waltz by Chopin, while we women tidied up in the dining room. His beautiful hands on the keyboard and his open smile are the last memories I have of my cousin-brother. We went to bed unaware of the tragedy that loomed before us.

At six in the morning the SS rang the doorbell. I knew it was them from the unexpected sound that woke me with a start, and without a moment's hesitation I got out of bed, whispering to mother and Piera, "I can't bear to hear those footsteps again," and went out on the balcony. That hangman's step decided my life in that instant. In my nightgown I flattened myself against the wall with my ear to the crack of the balcony door to hear what was happening inside. But what was happening? A hard voice was saying, "Kommt! Kommt!" and right away the window behind me was closed from the inside: my mother wanted to save at least me. The voices were more muffled now, but I heard my mother exclaim, "My Carlo, I'll never see him again!" And then the agitated voice of Aunt Alba, "No, I am not going to take my fur coat. We're not going to the theater!" I couldn't not understand, but my brain and my limbs were immobilized. I can still see the building opposite ours, a window opening and a woman completely oblivious shaking a rag from it and down below at the tobacco shop a line forming of people waiting for the store to open to pick up their daily ration of ciga-rettes. My eyes saw these things, while my heart and my ears tried to perceive each sound that came from the house.

The balcony I was on was long and narrow and it had two entrances, the one I had used to come out and one from the kitchen, which was still closed. At a certain point I heard it open but nobody came out. The voice of the German became more dis-tinct, more pressing: "Kommt, kommt!" Then there was the sound of the apartment door closing and, cutting through the silence, several turns of the key in the lock. Then nothing. I waited some more, I don't know how long, perhaps just a few seconds; time didn't mean anything to me anymore. I went back into the empty, indescribably disheveled house through the kitchen entrance (I learned later that it had been Giorgio who had opened it for me, having guessed my hiding place). Only a quarter of an hour had gone by, the longest one of my life, and the longer I live the more I am ashamed of it. I ran to the door: it was locked and could be opened only with the keys. I wanted to leave immediately, thinking that the Germans would come back to loot the apartment. I went back into the room where I had slept and began tying knots in the sheets to lower myself down from the little balcony where I had been hiding, onto the large one beneath it. I was still in my nightgown; I had to get dressed. Among my clothes, hung over a chair the night before, I found the keys to the house. Aunt Alba, even in that frantic quarter of an hour, had found the time to think of leaving me the keys.

I wouldn't be needing the knotted sheets now—I could leave faster by the door, fast enough to go look for my father. When I closed the door behind me, the door of the apartment on the other side of the landing opened. The family of Baron Sava, awakened by the unusual noise, had looked on helplessly through the keyhole and when they saw me alone they flung the door open to offer their help. I just asked if I could phone my father and I told him to leave the pension immediately, I would come meet him. He didn't understand, but how could he? He thought that we, too, had been advised to leave the house; he left without waiting for me. My host insisted on falsifying my identity card, just in case; instead of Levi I became Levigati, and he told me how to get to piazza Fiume by tram. My father was not waiting outside the door of the pension. I went upstairs and learned from Signora Mortara that he had gone to via de Pretis, to an old comrade from the First World War who had offered him a job.

It was a quarter past seven. I gave Signora Mortara a two-second account of the tragedy and begged her to leave her house immediately as well, as I had already done earlier when I phoned. "I'm over eighty years old. What are they going to do to me?" she said. But she listened to me and she made it just in time because at nine o'clock they knocked on her door, too.

I was back on my way, this time on foot, looking for via de Pretis, with no idea of the number and unable to remember the name of my father's friend. The only thing I remembered was that he had an only daughter who was fourteen years old and whose name was Nanù. My legs carried me forward, but when I stopped to ask directions at the corner of via 4 Fontane, I realized that my voice wasn't working. I remember the shocked look on the face of the woman I was speechlessly trying to talk to. I walked by the Ministry of Police at Palazzo Viminale, where some empty trucks with just a few SS men on board were starting to move out; I thought that maybe they were going out on more raids. When at last I arrived at via de Pretis I was about to go into the first doorway to ask the concierge if a fourteen-year-old

girl named Nanù lived there when I looked up to see my father. I
still had the strength to respond to his questioning smile. He was
waiting for his friend. I told him we had to go upstairs. "At eight
o'clock in the morning? We can't bother people at such an early
hour!" He realized that I was petrified and he followed me up.
When at last the elevator door had closed, as we were on our way
to the top floor, the terrible story came out, and telling it made it
become reality in my mind: "We're all alone, just you and I."

THE LEVIS whom the Germans picked up at 21 via
Flaminia were taken to the military college in via della
Lungara, whose huge, empty rooms were gradually filling
up with the people arrested that morning. Alberta's
mother and Piera, however, were not on any of the lists
of Roman Jews, and when a voice announced, "All
Catholics from mixed marriages move into the next
room," Aunt Alba convinced them to step forward, even
though the voice immediately added that, if anyone was
discovered attempting to pass himself off as Catholic, ten
Jews would be killed on the spot. While they were waiting
to be interrogated, mother and daughter worked out their
answers. Piera went to the bathroom, hoping to throw
their identity cards down the toilet, but the toilets were
blocked up so, tearing the cards into minuscule pieces, she
ate their names and photographs. That afternoon they

told Hauptsturmführer Dannecker, who interrogated them with the help of a bilingual prisoner, that they were from Bologna and had lost everything, including their papers, in the terrible bombing of September 25 that had almost destroyed the city. They were Catholics, Piera declared, her mother Aryan and she the daughter of a mixed marriage. They were in Rome only because they had nothing left, not even a roof over their heads, and had asked for hospitality from the relatives of her father.

They were believed. Hurriedly they abandoned their suitcase with the few things gathered together during the morning's panic. Outside they found themselves in the middle of the street just before curfew. Overwhelmed with anxiety, they made it to the house of the wartime comrade, where they found Alberta and her father and where they stayed for a few days, until they were able to obtain false identity cards.

I TRIED for a long time to find out about the fate of Signora Della Seta. Nobody returned to the apartment in via Flaminia and it was sold. The Della Setas deported to Auschwitz were quite numerous and I didn't know her first name. At last, when I'd lost all hope, I found her. In that October of 1943 Eva Della Seta found refuge together with her brother in a villa they had in Chianni, in the province of Pisa, and they were joined there by other members of the family. They were eight people in all, including a sixteen-year-old boy. Someone in the town betrayed them or perhaps sold them to pocket the few thousand lire their lives were worth. There are no survivors to tell the story. On April 20, 1944, presumably at dawn, they were picked up and taken to a jail in Florence. From Florence, on an unknown date, they were transferred to the concentration camp at Fòssoli, in the province of Modena, where Signora Della Seta turned fifty-nine on May 10. On the fifteenth, the commandant of the camp, Karl Titho, ordered the prisoners to get ready to leave Fòssoli the next morning. "Finally," he said, "the order to depart has arrived. You will work in Germany for the great German effort, for the final victory."

The train, made up of a large number of freight cars with straw spread on the floor, left Florence on May 16. The journey is recounted by a man named Keller, one of the guards who accompanied the convoy. It is part of the deposition he gave at the trial of Friedrich Bosshamer, the SS officer responsible for the deportations from Italy:

East of Munich the convoy made a fairly long stop for the first time. We had been traveling without interruption for ten to twelve hours. . . . The occupants of the cars were made to get off in turns, car by car, to see to their needs. They were forced to do it there on the tracks, which, in the end, were completely *filthy. . . . Food was also distributed, again for the first time. . . . After Munich, food was distributed another couple of times. . . . Later on, at Frontleitstellen, we procured some hot soup, which was then distributed in the cars. They could only take care of their needs, however, during the stops and these happened often, at least once a day. . . . Up to the unloading in Auschwitz the journey lasted at least four days [*in reality it lasted five*]. . . . When we arrived in the vicinity of Auschwitz, the tracks were full of other convoys. We were stopped all night near the unloading dock of the camp before we could pull up to it. The train stayed at the ramp one entire day and night before being able to unload. We—that is, the* Bergleitkommando—*had plenty of time to see the other trains being unloaded and to observe the procedures that followed. They were trains full of Jews from Hungary and Holland. The openings of the freight cars were closed up with wire. The people in the cars must have been terribly thirsty because I could see them sticking their hands out between the strands of wire to catch the drops of rain—the weather was horrible—that were running off the roofs of the cars.*

Our Transportführer *called out attention to the procedures followed by the other trains after unloading. He was horrified and said that it was a disgrace. After he told me about it, I saw how the occupants of a convoy from Hungary were pulled down off the trains by prisoners of the camp armed with clubs and how some of these prisoners literally threw old people and children out of the cars. Then I saw that they made them go in groups into a place nearby, where several SS officers in long capes used sticks to divide the Jews into two groups and, as was abundantly clear, to send off to one side men and women who looked young and strong and to the other old people and children. It was evident that the first group consisted of people who looked like they could work, while the other was made up of people who were less than fully capable. While the group of people capable of work was taken to the barracks, the others were led on in groups toward an enormous structure with great iron doors that opened and closed automatically.*

Prisoners from the camp pushed and shoved the Jews into that place and hit them with clubs. The Jews let out high-pitched screams and shouts of pain. At the sight of this I made my way over to the great doors and was able to observe that more and more Jews were being forced into the space while the Jews already inside were undressing or were already naked. . . . I later learned from prisoners of the camp who served as guards that the great room was a gas chamber in which the Jews, after the women's hair was cut off, were killed with gas. . . . At the time so many trains arrived each day that they were scarcely able to gas the prisoners and burn the bodies in the crematoria behind the gas chambers, and some of the bodies had to be burned with flamethrowers. . . . Some of the sick people taken from the trains were left to lie all night on the ramp and on the tracks. Nobody looked after them and when, the next morning, they came to take them away they were almost all dead already. Our train was unloaded in exactly the same way.

. . .

EVA DELLA SETA DI CAPUA presumably entered the gas chamber immediately after getting off the train on May 23, 1944.

GIORGIO LEVI, who would have turned seventeen in November, remained locked up in the military college in via Lungara until October 18, when, together with fifty other prisoners, he was put on one of the freight cars waiting on a track at the Rome-Tiburtina station. On the night of October 22, he arrived at Auschwitz-Birkenau, where the train remained stopped and sealed shut until dawn the next day. Selected for work along with another 149 deportees, he was tattooed with the number 15874. He died in an unknown location; there is no trace of him after December 29, 1943.

Mario Levi was fifty-five years old and he arrived at Auschwitz on the night of October 22, 1943, in the same car as his wife and son. But what happened to him after that is unclear. He, too, died in an unknown place on an unknown date.

Alba Ravenna Levi was fifty-two years old. Deported to Auschwitz with her husband and son, she died in the gas chamber immediately upon arrival, on October 23, 1943.

. . .

AFTER THE WAR, in 1954, Pius XII was the hero of a film entitled *Pastor Angelicus* produced by the Catholic Film Center in Gedda. The film recounts in emphatic tones and beautiful images moments in the life of the pope, who, as stated in the credits, is the Angelic Shepherd announced in medieval prophecy. The film is a cavalcade of pictures and music in which the war looks like a strange and supernatural force, a firestorm without heroes or villains.

Rome, March 25, 1997

NOTES

Bibliographic sources are given for quotations which appear in the text without specific references.

Page   *1936*
17   **"to make reparation . . . for the injustices"** in
           Giovanni Miccoli, *Santa Sede e Chiesa italiana di fronte
           alle leggi antiebraiche del 1938* (Milan, 1977) p. 183.

           1938
28   **"that the Church will never regret"** in Henri
           Fabre, *L'eglise catholique face au fascism et au nazisme*
           (Brussels, 1995), and cited in Georges Passelecq and
           Bernard Suchecky, *The Hidden Encyclical of Pius XI*
           (New York, 1997), pp. 102–3.
38   **"a segregation or distinction"** in Renzo De
           Felice, *Storia degli ebrei italiani sotto il fascismo* (Turin,
           1988), p. 324.

44   **"Suffered? No, it didn't suffer"** in Giorgio Israel, *Politica della razza e persecuzione antiebraica nella comunita scientifica italiana,* Conference on the Fiftieth Anniversary of the Racial Laws (Rome, 1989), p. 123.

47   **"Unfortunately there is something much worse"** in Miccoli, *Santa Sede e Chiesa italiana di fronte alle leggi antiebraiche del 1938,* p. 208, and Passelecq and Suchecky, *The Hidden Encyclical of Pius XI,* pp. 169.

49   **"Abel's sacrifice, Abraham's sacrifice"** The episode and quotations from the meeting with the Belgian Catholic pilgrims are cited in Miccoli, *Santa Sede e Chiesa italiana di fronte alle leggi antiebraiche del 1938,* p. 212, and Passelecq and Suchecky, *The Hidden Encyclical of Pius XI,* pp. 193–94.

51   **"With regard to domestic policy"** in *Balconi e cannoni. I discorsi di Mussolini,* film, L'Espresso-Instituto Luce, prt. 2.

52   **"I declare this pope"** in De Felice, *Storia degli ebrei italiani sotto il fascismo,* p. 303.

63   **"We know what happened yesterday"** in Passelecq and Suchecky, *The Hidden Encyclical of Pius XI,* p. 191.

64   **"The Holy Father has so many preoccupations"** in Jacques Nobècourt, *Le Vicaire et l'Histoire,* Editions du Seuil (Paris, 1964), p. 175.

1939

74   **"The press is capable of saying"** in Pietro Scoppola, *La Chiesa e il fascismo,* Laterza (Bari, 1973), p. 338.

74–75   **"the enemy of the cross"** in Passelecq and Suchecky, *The Hidden Encyclical of Pius XI,* p. 201.

75   **"I sit here and"** in Rolf Hochhuth, *The Deputy,* Richard Winston and Clara Winston, trs. (New York, 1963), p. 355.

79   **"The Church is being persecuted in Barcelona."**
        in Hugh Thomas, *The Spanish Civil War* (New York,
        1964).

        1940–43

103   **"Those under thirty-five years old"** in Andrea
        Riccardi, *Il potere del Papa da Pio XII a Paolo VI,* Laterza
        (Bari, 1988).

105   **"In a Christian state"** in Hochhuth, *The Deputy,*
        p. 386.

110–11 **"Still, in the darkness"** in Saul Friedlander, *Pope
        Pius XII and the Third Reich* (New York, 1980, reprint
        of 1966 ed.) p. 81.

122   **Letter of Adam Sapieha.** Statement of Father Pirro
        Scavizzi, in *Pio XII mi ha detto* (Rome, 1964);
        reprinted in *Il Tempo,* June 1, 1986.

126   **"My sermon will be short"** Like the other protests
        by the French clergy in July 1942, this is taken from
        Friedlander, *Pope Pius XII and the Third Reich,*
        pp. 114–15.

147   **"How do you think the Holy See"** in Liliana Pic-
        ciotto Fargion, *Il libro della memoria* (Milan, 1991),
        p. 817.

147–48 **"As soon as the Holy See"** in De Felice, *Storia degli
        ebrei italiani sotto il fascismo,* p. 478.

165–70 **"Uncle Mario, in a letter he sent"** in Alberta
        Temin Levi, unpublished manuscript.

172   **"Finally, the order to depart has arrived"** in Far-
        gion, *Il libro della memoria* (Milan, 1991), p. 857.

172–74 **"East of Munich"** in Fargion, *Il libro della memoria,*
        pp. 857–59.

SELECTED BIBLIOGRAPHY

Bensoussan, Georges. *Histoire de la Shoah*. Paris: Presse Universitaire de France, 1996.

Campus, Gianni. "Il treno di Piassa Giudia" in *La deportazione degli ebrei di Roma*. Cuneo: edizioni L'Arciere, 1995.

Centro Furio Jesi, ed. *Le menzogne della Rassa. Documenti e immagini del razzismo e antisemitismo fascista*. Bologna: Grafis editori, 1994.

Churchill, Winston. *The Second World War*. Boston: Houghton Mifflin, 1952 (reissue 1986).

Conference on the Fiftieth Anniversary of the Racial Laws. *La legislazione antiebraica in Italia e in Europe*. Rome: Chamber of Deputies, 1989.

De Felice, Renzo. *Storia degli ebrei italiani sotto il fascismo*. Turin: Einaudi, 1988.

Fabre, Henri. *L'église catholique face au fascism et au nazisme*. Brussels: Henri Fabre et Editions EPO, 1995.

Fargion, Liliana Picciotto. *Il libro della memoria*. Milan: Mursia, 1991.

Hilberg, Raul. *The Destruction of European Jews.* New York: Holmes & Meier, 1985.

Nastasi, Pietro. *Giornate di Storia della Matematica.* Conference proceedings, Hotel San Michele, Cetraro. 8–12 September, 1988. Unpublished manuscript, Department of Mathematics, Palermo.

———. *La Communita matematica italiana di fronte alle leggi razziali.* Unpublished manuscript, Department of Mathematics, Palermo.

Passelecq, Georges; Suchecky Bernard; Fennel, Steven, tr. *The Hidden Encyclical of Pius XI.* New York: Harcourt Brace, 1997.

Sarfatti, Michele. "Mussolini contro gli ebrei," in *Cronaca dell'elaborazione delle leggi del 1938.* Turin: Silvio Zamorani editore, 1994.

ACKNOWLEDGMENTS

I wish to express my gratitude to the staff of the Centre de Documentation Juive in Paris for their kindness and valuable assistance in tracking down various texts. Special thanks as well to the Centro Culturale ebraico of Rome, and to Benny Lai, Pietro Scoppola, Adriano Prosperi, Frediano Sessi, Carrado Vivanti, Pier Vittorio Ceccherini, Susanna Siberstein, Ivette and Giacomo Sabban, Mirella Tagliacozzo Calo, Alberta Temin Levi, and Rosetta Ajo Sermoneta.

INDEX